TSUNAMI OF
NETWORKERS

TSUNAMI OF NETWORKERS

Riding the biggest wave of the 21st Century, here's a
practical business handbook for sure-shot success
in Network Marketing; written by the author
having 20 years of experience in the
same Industry

By

MANOJ KUMAR

White Falcon Publishing

www.whitefalconpublishing.com

Tsunami of Networkers
Manoj Kumar

www.whitefalconpublishing.com

Requests for permission should be addressed to
E-mail: info@quirkypro.com
Website: www.quirkypro.com

ISBN - 978-93-89530-48-3

This book is dedicated to my beloved mother Late Smt. Gian Bala who imbibed in me success principles and attitude of 'self-belief', 'self-esteem', 'self-discipline' and 'winner always' right from my childhood.

Thank You and Love You dear Mom!

Preface

Tsunami of Networkers is the book written for all those who are in the Network Marketing Business or aspiring to be in. The book has been written by the author having 20 years of experience in building a profitable and sustainable business. This isn't a theoretical book rather a hands-on experience that the author has amassed over the years.

Every time I get down from the stage after delivering my talk, I'm greeted by an enthusiastic group of leaders appreciating my talk. The biggest compliment that I get is when they say that all the new people who attended my presentation will surely sign up. To me, this is immensely satisfying and a way of giving back. Many leaders insisted me to pen down my experiences for the benefit of a much wider audience not having access to my talks.

Having started my journey as a lecturer of Mathematics, teaching runs through my veins. I know, to become a good teacher, you first need to be a good student. When I came to this business, I became a student here. I attended countless seminars and business presentations and never went in without a diary and pen and always took notes. In my long and fruitful career of 20 years and still counting, I've accumulated rich experience and knowledge listening to the leaders of the Network Marketing Business.

Being an avid reader, I've *read* a number of books on different topics such as Leadership, Goals, Building Teams and Sales by renowned authors. They all enriched my knowledge and coached me in building my business to a sizeable level.

Somehow, I always felt the need of an authentic book which contains all the syllabus or steps of building the Network Marketing Business at one place. I found none. The business information was available in bits and pieces in different books. Also, there was no one who had written a book on this subject after being successful in the business. To me, this was an unchartered territory. I decided to sail in and write this book so that it becomes helpful to the flux of Networkers who are getting into this field. This book will be an effective business building tool for all of them.

Tsunami of Networkers is a book for those who want to do the business the right way and succeed. I would be selfish if the benefit of investment of my time in understanding and applying the success principles doesn't reach many. The concepts, steps and principles that I'm sharing with you through this book are being followed by successful leaders across all those countries in all the five continents where Network Marketing Business is a big success.

I'm sure this book will be ready-to-read handbook in your hands and guide you towards a successful career in Network Marketing. I wish you success. God bless!

Contents

Introduction

You can count the number of seeds in an apple. Cut the apple and count the seeds, but you can't count the number of apples in one seed.

The seeds for the Network Marketing Business in India have been sown and the saplings have come out. Experts say that the seeds are of top quality and the soil is perfect for a bumper crop for generations to come.

India is a young country with more than 70 crore youth raring to go. While most other nations of the world are getting older, India is beaming with youthfulness. This is a welcome sign for a vibrant nation. Entrepreneurship is the buzz of the town. Network Marketing Businesses are helping millions of youngsters by providing them an opportunity wherein they can create a long-term, permanent, and profitable business for themselves.

You remember that mathematical puzzle wherein flowers in a pond are doubling every day. If the whole pond is filled with flowers in 30 days, how much has the pond filled on the 29th day?

The answer is on the 29th day, the pond is just half filled. Because the flowers are doubling every day, the rest will be filled in just one day. That is the power of compounding.

Though Network Marketing Companies have been operational in India since the year 1995, but the guidelines from the Ministry of Consumer Affairs, Government of India, came only in the year 2016. There's going to be an explosive growth both in terms of new companies and young entrepreneurs choosing Network Marketing as a career. All the qualities and ingredients that are required for developing a profitable, long-term, and sustainable Network Marketing Business are present here in this country. This is a tidal wave that will create a 'Tsunami of Networkers'.

Why this book

The purpose of writing this book is to give this ' Tsunami of Networkers' a direction because force applied without direction isn't of much use. This book will provide them the step by step guidelines in building a successful business. This is a ready-to-read business handbook in a simple and lucid language, providing 20 years of rich and practical experience of the author.

This book has been written to benefit all the people who have dared to dream big and create permanent cash flow in their lives, enabling them to fulfil their dreams and goals. There's hardly any other book available that contains specific material written for Network Marketing Businesses. This book will fill that vacuum by providing complete guidance to the business owners on how to proceed in the business in a systematic manner by avoiding mistakes and applying the success principles that are being followed by successful networkers the world over.

I'm sure, this book will be a useful tool in your hands and in your organisation. For new people, this book will serve as a ready-reckoner covering all the aspects of the business from the very beginning. This book will also help in setting up agenda for your team meetings, PASE meetings and other business forums by providing you logical content in a sequential manner.

How to maximize your results from this book

For your comfort, I have divided the book into five sections. There are eleven chapters in all. Each section has the inclusion of meaningful chapters, and each chapter discusses in detail the purpose for which it has been written.

As you begin reading this book, highlight the areas that attract you the most. At the end of each chapter, I have purposely left one blank page for you to make notes. I am sure the content of this book is so useful and engaging that you will come back many times to read the chapters again and refer to the notes. At the end of each chapter, I have given points to summarize and recapitulate.

Promote this book to all the new persons joining your business. This book will help in laying a strong foundation, and you know, you can build a huge network if the foundation is strong.

You can also leave this book with your prospects as a follow-up tool. The prospects will surely get an insight as to why they should join the Network Marketing Business. This book will reduce your workload by putting the correct information in front of them, enabling them to make the right decision.

In the end, I pray to God that the knowledge that you gain from reading this book helps millions around the world in creating financial stability in their lives by building a successful Network Marketing Business. Happy Reading...

I wish you success!!

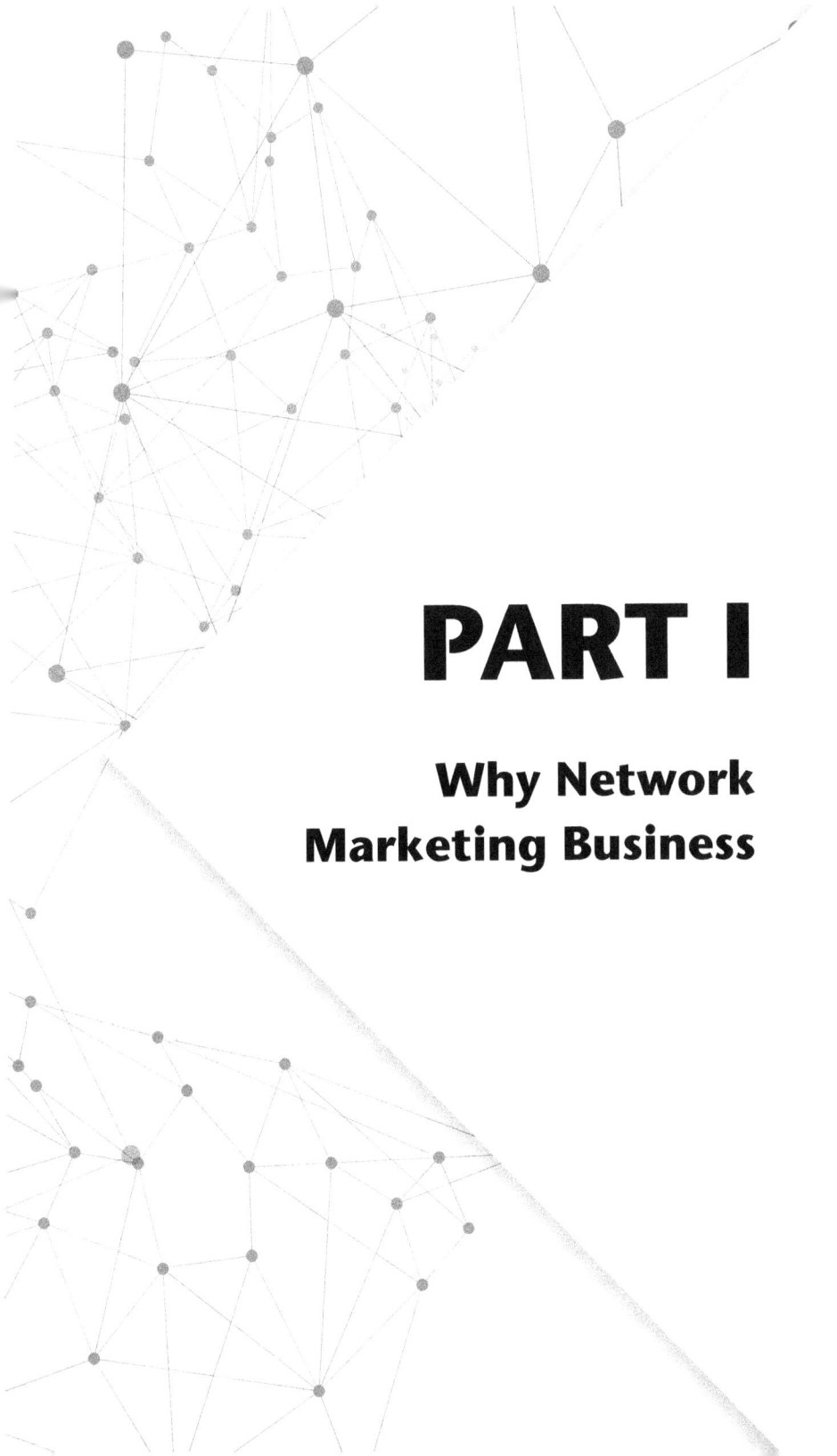

PART I

Why Network Marketing Business

CHAPTER 1

Roller-Coaster Ride for Network Marketing Businesses

It's been a big roller-coaster ride, but that makes it that much sweeter. We've been through a lot of ups and downs. That's what perseverance and mental toughness are all about: how you respond to negative times.

- MARK LORETTA

In the 20th century, thanks to the Industrial Revolution, world witnessed emergence of Industrial Age. Big companies in the field of Automobile, Steel and Computers dominated the corporate world. Globally, big wealth was controlled by big industries during that period. New machines to run the factories were invented and people who learnt to run those machines and factories were hired by factory owners. Job is basically the by-product of Industrial Revolution.

Automobile is considered as the first trillion-dollar trend when one American, Henry Ford, dreamt that every American could have a car. He incorporated the first biggest automobile company in the world to fulfil that dream. The Computer is considered the second trillion-dollar revolution. Now, computer is a household name. Computers have impacted us more than any other invention. Diversified use and application of this machine in all aspects of human life has been a remarkable achievement.

These dream-oriented industries provided jobs to millions of people. Many big companies that we see today were started around that period of time.

> ➢ Remember that people who know why to do a thing would always employ people who know how to do that thing.

Setting the Stage for Network Marketing Business

In the beginning of the 21st Century, with the rise of Internet, we moved into a new age known as the Information Age. Communication and Data are the products of the

Information Age. Big companies like Apple, Facebook, Google, Amazon and Twitter have completely transformed this age from Industrial to Information age. These companies have impacted the world in a big way. Networks replaced Factories and Consumers replaced Machines. Globe began to shrink.

The concept of building and owning huge networks have completely transformed the business perspective and distribution of wealth. WhatsApp, Facebook and Instagram are few examples of disrupters who have built big networks in comparatively lesser time.

If you understand and follow global trends, it is apparent that there has never been a better time to build your own business than now. The biggest contention is to catch the trends at an early stage.

➢ Are you ready to take advantage of this growing trend of Network Marketing Business?

Franchising Model

In the 1950s, the world witnessed arrival of the franchising model of business which was different from the traditional model. New terms of franchisor and franchisee were added in the business directory. Initially objected as being a fraud and a scam, eventually, it went on to become one of the most successful business models in the world.

Today, more than 63% of the businesses in the world are based on the franchising model. The success of franchising model led to further brainstorming by people to improve it further.

Just like Windows evolved as an improvement over DOS (Disc Operating System) in computers, Network Marketing came into existence as an improvement over the franchising model. If you study the franchising model, it is a single level marketing with one franchisor having a number of franchisees and the former having complete control over the number of franchising.

> Franchising model brought to the world the concept of time compounding. This one principle has completely transformed the modern business thinking.

Network Marketing is multi-level marketing and here, everyone has an opportunity to become a franchisor for one's own business and create multiple layers of the network. Frankly speaking, multi-level marketing is an advanced and improved version of single-level marketing and it has the potential of creating huge businesses all over the world.

In the 1960s and 70s, many Network Marketing Companies commenced operations in the United States and within a few years, they started growing up considerably. Steadily, their operations expanded to Asian countries and other continents of the world and grew significantly. Many professionals got attracted to such businesses because they could use the principle of time compounding here and create massive businesses for themselves.

Network Marketing in India

In India, towards the end of the last century, many Network Marketing Companies started their operations. Some of them were reputed international companies which started their operations in India. There were also a few Indian business houses who incorporated their own Network Marketing Companies by following a successful and proven international business model.

In the initial years, these companies had to face tremendous rejection and litigation. People were apprehensive of the success of such business models in India. It is quite obvious and natural. I will explain this in detail in Chapter 2 of this book through the **'Adoption Curve Model'** as to how people adapt to changes and innovation in business and technology. I am sure, it will unfold a new perspective of looking at the business of Network Marketing.

Why Network Marketing Business

Network Marketing is the simplest way of building your own network and make it big for yourself. It's the biggest business opportunity of the 21st Century. Network Marketing is a form of direct selling which has attracted people from all walks of life to get into it and grow significantly to fulfil their desired goals. Today, this business model is running successfully in all the continents of the world and Asia in particular.

Global data depicts that in the last one decade, job-cuts are more than job-opportunities. Disruptions are taking place in all industries and new structural dimensions are being added to the functioning of the businesses. Entrepreneurship is the buzzword in society.

> ➤ I always say that owning the smallest business is better than the biggest job because, in business, you can take your own decisions and chalk out your success journey.

Government is making a strong pitch for entrepreneurship development. Replacement of jobs is only possible when people get an alternative source of generating income. Entrepreneurship is the solution. Network Marketing is an alternative which can solve this problem. Network Marketing Business can provide decent incomes to people and solve the problem of the Government. Network Marketing can offer an attractive business opportunity to create a permanent cash flow for yourself and your generations to come.

Riding the Bumpy Road

Network Marketing Companies in India had to face a lot of heat during the initial years of their inception. There was no legal framework and legislation available for them. Even those who were getting into these companies were sceptical about their existence and survival. These companies lived on the peril of being declared fraudulent.

A lot of stir and confusion was created when many illegitimate companies came up in the garb of chit fund schemes, Ponzi schemes and pyramid schemes. These companies looted the hard-earned money of the people who were falsely trapped into such businesses. In the absence of an Act or guidelines from the Government relating to Direct Selling, such fraudulent companies created a bad name for the industry. Many such frauds and scams came to the forefront and Government had to take stern action against them.

Network Marketing Companies come under the purview of the Direct Selling Industry in India. Indian Direct Sellers Association (IDSA) is an autonomous body which acts as an interface and catalyst between Industry and the Government. IDSA continued its efforts to persuade the Government to come up with an Act safeguarding the interest of the legitimate Direct Selling Companies.

Many reputed companies doing legitimate business were implicated under an age-old act and went through a tough time. There was a growing need for legal demarcation between legal and illegal companies.

Guidelines for Direct Selling Industry by Government of India

Much to the respite of the Industry, in the year 2016, **Ministry of Consumer Affairs, Government of India** introduced guidelines for Direct Selling Industry, thereby paving way for the smooth functioning of the Network Marketing Companies. The Ministry also directed the State Governments to implement the guidelines in their respective states to create a conducive environment for legitimate direct sellers to function freely. Many State Governments have implemented the guidelines issued by the Government.

This step by the Government was welcomed by IDSA as a step in the right direction. The guidelines also laid to rest the future of chit fund and Ponzi schemes that had mushroomed in the marketplace. Direct Selling Companies welcomed and applauded the step taken by the Government. The Companies said that the guidelines will weed out fraudulent companies and protect consumer interests and motivate serious players to function in a free and fair way.

➢ It's considered a watershed moment for the Direct Selling Industry in India. Many new companies are now starting operations after gaining confidence from the steps taken by the Government.

Guidelines-The Game Changer

These guidelines created an environment of trust and belief for Network Marketing Companies. They started investing in infrastructure development. Since 2016, many new companies have come into existence.

I'm sure that in the coming years, many business houses of repute will adopt this channel of sales and get into Network Marketing Business. Also, the thrust by the Government for entrepreneurial development under Skill India Program is a motivating factor.

Just imagine the fact that even in the absence of any appropriate legislation, the industry crossed 1 billion dollars business. Obviously, with the Government guidelines in stride, it is a thriving business proposition.

> ➢ There's going to be a Tsunami of Networkers in India who will get opportunities in these companies to build big businesses for themselves.

FICCI-KPMG Report on the Contribution of Direct Selling to building India

Right around the time when Government came out to the rescue of Direct Selling Industry and published guidelines for direct selling companies doing legitimate business; in the corporate world leading firm **KPMG**, a global network of professional firms providing Audit, Tax and Advisory services together with **FICCI** (Federation of Indian Chamber of Commerce and Industry) brought out a report on *'The Contribution of Direct Selling to building India.'*

This report couldn't have come at a better time for the industry and is considered as an icing on the cake.

The FICCI-KPMG report stated that the Direct Selling Industry has the potential to reach revenues of Rs. 64,500 crores by the year 2025 from its current level of Rs. 7500 crores. It further projected that the industry can create potential employment for about 18 million people across India.

The report highlighted that the industry empowers women with nearly 60% of direct sellers being women. You can read the full report on the following weblink:

https://assets.kpmg/content/dam/kpmg/in/pdf/2016/12/Direct-2016.pdf

The report further stated that the industry is participating significantly in building India by contributing to various Government schemes such as Skill India, Make in India, Women Empowerment and Startup India.

Many Network Marketing Companies have built state of the art manufacturing units in India under Make in India mission of the Government and raised employment for local communities. They are providing business to many startups in logistics and supply chain management.

> ➤ In all, it's clearly visible that Network Marketing is the business to be in. It's the right time and we are in the right country. India is a young country with the largest youth power in the world.

Future of Network Marketing in India

Network Marketing Business is the fastest growing business of the 21st Century in the entire world. In the context of the Indian market, this business has great potential and scope.

With the strong guidelines of the Government and conducive work environment, this business is going to create many millionaire entrepreneurs in India.

As the Report of FICCI-KPMG suggests that there is going to be a huge upsurge in the revenues of such companies in India; the stage is set for an explosive growth in this field.

Friends, I have seen all this happening right in front of my eyes. Ever since I got into this business in the year 2000, I've been a witness to all these roller-coaster rides taking place in the Indian market. However, I withstood my ground firmly. I knew that I was in the right business at the right time and with the right people.

I had the privilege of meeting tens and thousands of people during the course of the last 20 years and I can tell you that this has been a very exciting and satisfying journey.

Today, when I look back, I find that decision to build this business has delivered fruits for me. I became a student of this business, learnt from my uplines and built huge teams in my network and thus enjoyed fruits of the business.

This business has taught me innumerable techniques, methods, principles and strategies and has also given me a platform to exhibit my capabilities in guiding, building, inspiring and motivating many teams.

> The FICCI-KPMG report stated that Direct Selling Industry has the potential to reach revenues of Rs. 64,500 crores by the year 2025 from its current level of Rs. 7500 crores. It further projected that the industry can create potential employment for about 18 million people across India. The report highlighted that the industry empowers women with nearly 60% of direct sellers being women.

I had the opportunity of meeting very successful business owners in this industry from all over the world who have built an empire for themselves in their respective countries. Leaders from US, Canada, Japan, Australia, Korea, China and Russia besides India have contributed significantly to my wisdom and helped me in creating a long term, profitable and sustainable business for myself and my family.

Here, I'm giving below some of the reasons for building the Network Marketing Business. Identify your own reasons to build this business.

Reasons Why Network Marketing is the Business of the 21st Century and why you should get in

Build a Business of Your Own

Do job-cuts worry you immensely? Do you feel underpaid yet overworked?

Here's a business which gives you an opportunity to be your own boss. Build it to create an asset for yourself. Today is the age of networking. It's one who owns the network makes money. You are either in someone's network or you have your own network. When you build a network, you increase your net worth.

It's a choice that you need to make. Network Marketing gives you an opportunity to build your own business by following a successful team who are more than willing to help you in teaching, guiding and mentoring.

➤ I always say, "Dig the 'well' when you're not thirsty because you can't dig the 'well' when you are thirsty." Build a pipeline of your own for a consistent cash flow.

Make your Wallet Fatty

As the standard of living is going up; so is the cost of living. With an increase in your family size or age, expenses are bound to rise. Have you ever wondered how will your present job increments meet these ever increasing expenses?

Network Marketing Business gives you a proven business model in which you can make a good amount of money by following the system. Build this business for two years with full commitment and hard work and it will ensure a steady cash flow for you and that too consistently rising.

Freedom to Work from Anywhere

This business gives you flexibility and freedom to build this business anytime anywhere. You can build this business from your home, build it part-time with low overhead cost and yet make it big. This is the reason this business attracts lots of women workforce.

Even if you're moving to some other state or locality, you need not start all over again. This business goes with you wherever you go. However, the same is not true in a job or traditional self-employed businesses. This is the inherent nature of this business. You can build a huge business with minimum overhead cost.

Ride the Boom of Social Media and Internet

Social Media is the biggest game-changer for the Network Marketing business globally. As we are living in the Information Age, internet and social media can help us connect with our prospective clients in a faster and professional manner.

Do you use social media only for socializing or you want to use it to build your business?

Learn techniques of using social media and internet in this fast-changing world to keep pace with technology and build big teams all over the world. Take help of the social media apps like Facebook, Instagram, etc. to spread your reach to those places where you haven't gone so far.

GOOD (Get out of Debt)

Nowadays, people are trapped in debt because of inflation and the rise in the cost of living. This is not a good situation to be in. This is a vicious circle and once trapped, it is extremely difficult to get out of it. Build this business to get out of debt and live a life without debt. It's a great feeling. This business provides a systematic plan to help you build your financial stability.

Follow successful uplines in your business to build a business which provides you ample room to live a debt-free life. "Never spend the money that you don't own" is the fundamental principle of remaining debt-free. Build a cash flow which will take care of the additional cost of living, thus, making life stress free.

Live a Life of Significance

Network Marketing Business gives you an opportunity to significantly influence the lives of those who come in your teams by virtue of leading, counselling and mentoring them. When you make a positive impact in someone's life, it gives you immense pleasure and happiness.

You live a life of significance when many lives are better off because of you. When you succeed personally, it is a very happy and proud moment for you, but when someone you help becomes successful, it is very satisfying and a moment of pride for you. This business is based on the principle of helping others grow.

Become a Magnetic Leader

In Network Marketing, you build and mentor big teams. First you become a player, then a captain and finally a coach. Initially, when you enter this business, you are a team player and learn how to be a good one. Steadily as you grow, you have a team and you start learning leadership traits.

When you successfully guide and mentor teams, you become a role model for them. They want to emulate you. Thus, you become a magnetic personality. This transition is automatic in Network Marketing Business. This business teaches you the basic principle of **Learn, Teach and Teach Others to Teach.**

Rewards and Recognitions

Besides making a lot of money, there are wonderful Rewards and Recognition that one gets once being successful in Network Marketing Business. Many companies offer overseas trips to exotic locations for successful people in the business, creating lifetime memories.

You're adequately and ably rewarded for your performance and people appreciate from the core of their hearts when you achieve success in this business. You're celebrated on a big stage amongst thousands of people sitting in the audience. This is truly very inspiring and motivating. Your downlines want to emulate you, which is good for your business. You move from signatures to autographs.

Use Proven Expertise

In Network Marketing Business, you grow only when you help others to grow. It's a perfect win-win situation. You are assured of help by those who are already successful in the business. This is a unique combination. Just imagine is this possible in your job or traditional business?

Here, in this business, you have at your access, the experience of those, who are there where you want to reach. This makes your journey to success pretty convenient. You don't need to reinvent the wheel. Just follow the footsteps of the successful leaders as laid down in the system. By using their proven expertise, you grow in the business. This is called the principle of duplication.

Create a Legacy

Network Marketing Business gives you residual income which helps you create a legacy for your family. It is an asset that you can pass on to your generations. It gives you a sense of pride and achievement. Many have done this for their loved ones and they are willing to guide you.

You know, many traditional businesses die a natural death when the next generation does not want to pursue it further; hence there is no money any further. Here, in this business – you build it once, build it right and create a legacy for your generations to come. It is just like planting apple trees, the fruits are there for your loved ones even when you are not there.

Today I conduct Seminars, Webinars, Team Meetings, Product Sessions, One to One Counselling Sessions, Podcasts and Expert Speaker Program for my teams all over India and abroad. This business really makes you a celebrity and a magnetic personality.

Having invested a considerable period of time of my life in this business, I have gained immense knowledge and with all the wisdom that I have gained, I can say with full authority and confidence that **We Are Just Getting Started.**

> ➤ India will see a flux of Network Marketing Businesses getting started in years to come. Existing companies will see a considerable surge in their network and hence rising revenues.

These businesses will significantly impact in empowering the youth of India in building a successful future for themselves. I have reasons to prove it and will discuss the same with you in the subsequent chapters.

It's the right time to get started in this business and create a legacy for your family. If you're already in, **make it big guys!**

Just to recapitulate....

- It's been a Roller-Coaster ride for Network Marketing Business in India. IDSA persuaded the Government to bring requisite legislation for creating the right atmosphere for legitimate companies to operate.

- Network Marketing Business came into existence as an improvement over the franchising model, just like windows is an improvement over of DOS.

- Guidelines of the Ministry of Consumer Affairs (Government of India), in the year 2016, about direct selling businesses in India is a shot in the arm for IDSA and Network Marketing Business.

- It's a big game-changer for the functioning of the Network Marketing Companies in India contributing to various Government schemes such as Skill India, Make in India, Women Empowerment and Startup India.

- The FICCI-KPMG report on 'Contribution of Direct Selling to building India' stated that Direct Selling Industry has the potential to reach revenues of Rs. 64,500 crores by the year 2025 from its current level of Rs. 7500 crores.

- It further projected that the industry can create potential employment for about 18 million people across India. The report highlighted that the industry empowers women with nearly 60% of direct sellers being women.

- There are many reasons to build the Network Marketing Business in India. You need to identify why you would choose such business for yourself.

- This business gives you a platform to exhibit your talent and leadership skills. You can use the proven skills taught by leaders of the business and create a legacy for your family.

Scribble your Notes

CHAPTER 2

Understanding Waves and Adoption Curve

You can't stop the waves but
you can learn to surf.

-JON KABAT-ZINN

Paradoxical Encounter with Naysayers

Paradoxical Encounter with Naysayers
Many people, whom I meet these days, tell me that they had also seen this 'type' of business 20-25 years ago. A few of them said that they even got into it but quit after some time for various reasons. Knowing that I am successful in such business, they ask me swiftly, "Is this business the same as before?" I ask a very simple question to these people, "Do you see travel, IT or Computer industry same as it was 20-25 years ago?" The answer is a simple 'No'.

Every industry has risen tremendously in their own perspective and achieved bigger milestones by constantly upgrading on all fronts, be it infrastructure, technology, innovation or product design. It is equally true for Network Marketing Companies as well.

Understanding Waves

You need to ponder over this and understand the concept of waves and their impact over a period of time. You will realize the potential of the waves and their altitude. You will understand what would be the impact of its subsequent phases. With a boom in technology, Network Marketing is riding wave 4 in the 21st century. What people talk about seeing this business years ago was when it was in Wave 1 and 2. There has been a tremendous change over this period of time.

This young country, with Internet and Social Media in their hands, has created a new dimension to this business. Social Media is a boon for this business. It paves the way for catering to the needs of a larger audience beyond the frontiers of one nation and creating an explosion in the global arena. We're living in very exciting times. More and more people are excited to build huge networks across the globe with technology-driven techniques and achieve tremendous growth going forward.

> It's a tidal wave and you will see a Tsunami of Networkers creating big businesses in the 21ˢᵗ century. Young entrepreneurs will make use of this tide to interact and contact with prospective clients simply with a touch of a button.

This is a golden handshake between hi-tech and high-touch and will create millions of first-time Networkers embracing Network Marketing Business. These young minds will make use of this momentum and create massive businesses for themselves. You would see the magic of this wave happening in your life when you ride this wave and accelerate your business growth with the multiplier effect.

Let me explain this through the Adoption Curve.

The Adoption Curve is a bell-shaped curve which explains and shows the adoption of new ideas, innovation or industry by society through five different stages.

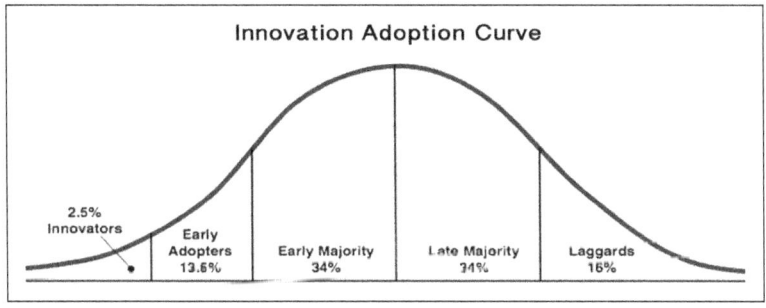

1. **Innovators**

   Innovators are the first ones who prefer to take risks by being the first in society to start new ideas, innovation and industry. They're quite impactful because of their high social value, income and financial stability. They're the early birds to adopt new technology and innovation. Innovators are just a small 2.5% in society. They see and understand the trend well before others have even a clue about it.

2. **Early Adopters**
Early adopters consist of a group of visionaries in society who adopt new innovations, ideas and industry. They constitute 13.5% of the whole society and comprise of young, educated and smartly groomed leaders.
They're also risk-takers who have deep influence over the community. They're the ones who provide technical advice and information that other adopters demand. Early adopters understand the influence and outcome of any innovation and they also fathom as to why innovators have got into it. They're great beneficiaries of the innovation, idea and industry.

3. **Early Majority**
This stream of people in the society are those individuals who take slightly longer time to adopt the changes but have a higher percentage (34% in numbers). They're the largest chunk of society who take advantage of the early adoption of an idea, innovation or industry. They are that curiosity group who would always weigh the features and benefits, likes and dislikes before adoption. They measure the pros and cons of every aspect before taking a final call. They're cautious with both their time and money before taking a decision to invest in the innovation. Early majorities are open-minded to listen to opinions of early adopters before forming their own opinion. Though they are not afraid of taking risks, they don't go out and search for it.

4. **Late Majority**

    They're fourth in the row and are 34% in the society to adopt. They adopt a change only when they see Early Majority and Early Adopters doing it before them. They will embrace the change post verification of the fact that the majority have adopted those innovative changes. When the education system is robust about innovation, they get influenced.

    They would resist change up to the point they can. They're a closed-minded group and stick to the perception without understanding the product and the innovation. They're usually convinced by close-knit family and friends.

5. **Laggards**

    Laggards are the late entrants consisting of 16% of the population. They will start using the technology and innovation only when the existing product with them becomes obsolete and redundant. They stick to the traditions and virtually are the last ones to adopt innovation. They're not big thinking group rather a bunch of satisfied groups. They incur losses due to this resistance. They're both closed-minded and having suspicious nature. They suspect innovators and adopters.

If we understand and evaluate the waves and adoption curve, we reach the conclusion that Network Marketing Industry, which started in the mid-Nineties towards the end of the last century, could barely reach up to the zone of Early Adopters and Early Majority in India due to the constant fear of survival and existence. This scepticism arrested their appetite for innovation.

It was only in the year 2016 that the industry got confidence when Government of India issued guidelines for Direct Selling Industry. Post 2016, there has been a surge in investments by existing companies.

> ➢ FICCI-KPMG report predicts that by the year 2025, the Direct Selling industry will reach a whopping 64500 crore rupees in revenues.

Now, Network Marketing is being taught as a subject in many universities across India. This is the place and the time of the tidal wave that I've discussed earlier and the Tsunami of Networkers that will create big momentum.

The scope

We're currently in the zone of Early Adopters and Early Majority. This wave will create a majestic influence on tech-savvy young people to get into this business. Many new companies will come into existence in this period to make use of this tidal wave. So, it is a very exciting time for all of us to be part of that explosive growth and have a decent share of the pie.

When people tell me that you're lucky that you started so early and made it big, they miss the bus again. For me, **we're just getting started in India and the best is yet to come.** These people need to understand that there's no better time to build this business than NOW.

I ask them a simple question, "Do you think driving on a highway in a luxurious car is exciting now or was 20 years ago?"

Twenty years ago, the highways weren't that well spread. There were no beautiful resorts and eateries along the way. Mobile phone technology was not that advanced, no GPS for navigation and no medical facilities in case of emergency. Most of the National and State highways were single lanes. Many parts of the highway were in bad shape and condition. Proper lighting along the roads was also not there.

Now, what we see is a completely different scenario. We've more powerful cars with navigation facilities inbuilt and soon Internet Cars are being launched. Every car manufacturer is trying to make your cabin experience better than before.

We have world-class National highways and better connecting State highways. We have beautiful malls, shopping centres, food joints and medical facilities. This has made long-driving comfortable, exciting and less time-consuming. On top of it, I feel it is just the beginning of the infrastructure development story. With the Government's infrastructure push, things are going to improve further.

Same applies to this business as well. Network Marketing Companies have just got a breather from Government and they have got to capitalize on this. It's time for these companies to scale up their business and provide their business owners with world-class infrastructure and best quality products and services. Companies are investing in building world-class plants, using modern technology and expertise to stay ahead in the competition.

Growing competition amongst Network Marketing Companies to provide better services and pay-out plans brings bright prospects on the table for business owners. I see many companies making significant value addition in marketing and compensation plans. This makes the game even more exciting.

The success of companies in the last few years has propelled other business houses to adopt the Network Marketing business model. I'm sure many are in the pipeline. When people tell me that there are so many network marketing companies, I reply back to them with greater vigour that it's because the business model is successful.

> **This wave will create a majestic influence on tech-savvy young people to get into this business. Many new companies will come into existence in this period to make use of this tidal wave. So, it is a very exciting time for all of us to be part of that explosive growth and have a decent share of the pie.**

While Network Marketing Businesses are growing by leaps and bounds, still there are people who can't see it and believe it. Have you ever wondered why? This is because they don't perceive any value in it and misread it as a product-selling business. Yes, products are important, but that's only one aspect of the business.

> ➢ The real power is in the network that channelizes products. It's people who move the products and not vice versa.

While many people who attend business plan meetings of any Network Marketing Company, come back and say they saw circles and circles on the board. What they don't comprehend is the lines between the circles binding them together.

> Money does not chase companies with good products and services, money chases great leaders dealing in those products and services.

It's not about products, it's about people. The success and popularity of Network Marketing Business have encouraged experts' world over to write and discuss about it in world-famous journals, magazines, TV shows and books.

We can easily predict the result and influence of the current wave 4 that Network Marketing Companies are riding on. This will have a multiplier effect and you will see tremendous growth happening in India. Network Marketing is no longer on trial rather it is a trusted and proven business in which thousands have achieved financial success. This profession is helping millions of people achieve greater success financially and they're chasing their dreams.

Choosing the Right Company

When you know this business has worked for many, this can work for you as well. Once you are willing to get into this business, the first and foremost important thing is to choose the right company to be in.

As told earlier, there are thousands of Network Marketing Companies operating in the country and many more are starting their operations, so how do you identify the right company for you where you can excel and fulfil your dreams and goals?

While innovators and Early Adopters had little choice to make, you have got a wider spectrum to select the company of your liking. However, the big question is how will you choose? What are the traits of a successful business? When every company boasts of being a great company with a wonderful compensation plan better than the other, how to identify the right company?

First of all, you need to be very careful about some bogus companies which are out there to swindle your money and waste time. These companies will offer you lucrative incentives, show you big dreams, make huge promises and tell you how quickly you can get there. You better be watchful of these scamsters. All it requires is a little research on your part to know the credentials and functioning of the company.

After all, it is a matter of your time, money and reputation. If you wish that your efforts should ably be rewarded and your future be secured, choose a company that has a proven track record and intends to be there in the market for the long-term.

Here are a few fundamental questions you need to get answers to while selecting the right company.

1. **Is the company around for some time?**

   Choose a company that has been there in the market for some time and people have achieved personal and financial success through that company. Ideally, the company should be there for at least five years or more.

   It's not advisable to work with a startup company unless factors are very compelling in terms of its promoters. In many cases, the businesses do not survive the first five years of starting. When a company is there in the market for a longer period of time, there are fewer chances of it being a bogus company.

2. **Do its promoters have credibility?**

   This is one of the most important checks for anyone who is willing to put their head down and start working with a company. This is important because the promoters are the ones who are guiding the ship and they know how to navigate the ship in troubled waters and stay on course.

   These people have a considerable amount of personal integrity and character at stake. Their decisions carry a lot of value. Once they decide to take people along, they will continue to do so both in good and bad times.

   Network Marketing companies had a tough time when there was no Government backing in place for them in terms of legislation or guidelines before the year 2016.

   Nevertheless, strong promoters sailed with confidence. They had the vision that things will be better as they were doing legitimate business and always believed that it was the right thing to do. No matter what the circumstances, they always cared for their business owners and continued to fight for their rights. So, always back a company that is run by promoters having strong credibility and vision going forward.

3. **Does the company have a good plan for business owners and is it permissible at law?**

   The company you intend to choose must have a solid plan of action for its distributors. Its business plan should be legally viable and should not promise quick-rich method and some tricks to make money. The company should be fundamentally strong with a strong foot forward in Network Marketing.

   Network Marketing is the business of the people and no company can do justice to its distributors if it is not clear of pursuing Network Marketing model which is proven and tested. The business plan and operations should be in line with the guidelines issued by the government in this regard. Also, ensure that the company is investing consistently in innovation, technology and infrastructure.

4. **Does the company offer a unique product line that can attract customers towards it?**
   Products are the backbone of any Network Marketing Company. Identify a company that has in its basket. products having unique features, usage and benefits and each product has a story associated with it.

   As a distributor, you should feel proud of explaining the products to your prospects and customers. When you like the products for their technology, uniqueness and usage, you can expect your network to duplicate you.

   So, identify the company that has products which your network will easily duplicate.

   The company should have a strong training team both online and classroom to guide you and your team about the products, their usage and benefits. The company should provide informative and presentable literature enabling you to use them to build your network.

5. **What is the Compensation Plan or Payout Plan of the company?**
   You are entering this business to make money and fulfil your dreams and goals. It will entirely depend on the payout plan that the company offers to you. You should understand the compensation plan of the company and see that it has the capacity to fulfil your dreams over a period of time. The payout plan should be clear

and distributor friendly. It should offer rewards to the distributors for performance and consistency.

6. **What kind of support system is there in terms of education, guidance and overall development?**

   This, to me, is the most important point to check before joining the business of any Network Marketing Company. Network Marketing is a long-term business and this business has got all the potential to transform you in all aspects of your life.

   This business, when rightly structured and built, will impact not only this generation of yours but the coming generations as well. This has happened to me and it can happen for you too.

   The biggest tool at your disposal for building a long term, sustainable and profitable business all over the world is the support system. I always say, "Systems work, people don't." The system includes your Sponsor, Upline team, Meetings and Seminars, Books, Audio and Video clips, Podcasts, Conference Calls and many other formal and informal associations.

   You need to select a company which offers you a system that focuses on regular training, teaching you skills to build this business and helping you grow both in terms of character and personality.

Friends, Network Marketing Business has tremendous potential to provide you with a platform where you can achieve your dreams and goals and at the same time, help others do the same. Choose your company wisely because your whole life can change if you choose the right one. You can do a lot of research and fact-checking for this. Get your facts right and take the right decision. There are many companies in the pipeline. Don't get distracted; take a firm call.

If you're already in the business of Network Marketing, stick to it. Keep your folks together. Be the right leader and mentor for them. This is the business of duplication. People don't do what you say, people do what you do. Take advantage of this tidal wave to build a solid business. Choose the right company and give yourself a time horizon of 3-5 years.

Just to recapitulate....

- Network Marketing is riding wave 4 in the 21st century. We're living in very exciting times as more and more people are excited to build huge networks across the globe with technology-driven techniques and achieve tremendous growth going forward.

- It's a tidal wave and what you will see is a tsunami of networkers creating big businesses.

- The Adoption Curve is a bell-shaped curve which explains and shows the adoption of new ideas, innovation or industry by society through five different stages namely – Innovators, Early Adopters, Early Majority, Late Majority and Laggards.

- The Wave Theory and Adoption Curve depict that Network Marketing Businesses have barely reached the zone of Early Adopters and Early Majority Stage in India. There is a huge untapped potential.

- FICCI-KPMG report predicts that by the year 2025, the Direct Selling industry will reach a whopping 64500 crore rupees in revenues. The success of companies in the last few years has propelled other business houses to adopt the Network Marketing business model.

- You need to be careful in choosing the right company. Do some fact-checking. If you are already in the business, build it ethically and only then you will be able to keep your folks together.

Scribble your Notes

CHAPTER 3

Traits of Successful Networkers

If your actions inspire others to
dream more, learn more, do more
and become more, you are a leader.

-JOHN QUINCY ADAMS

Success is never by chance; it's always by choice; you always choose to be successful. Success is a planned event.

Why is the Network Marketing the business of the 21st Century?

Because in this business, not only you succeed, but you help others to be successful as well. In fact, you succeed in this business only by helping your teams to succeed. This is a win-win formula. That's why people get attracted to it. In traditional business, you see corporate wars and boardroom strategies to bring other businesses down.

> Success has a peculiar phenomenon of leaving behind footprints; footprints that others can follow to become successful. Success breeds success.

Here, in this business, you uplift others to grow. When you succeed, your team gets motivated and they want to replicate you. When your team succeeds, you have greater success. This is the beauty of this business.

In this business, if someone in your team stands up and says that he/she wants to build a bigger business than you, it is a compliment and not a challenge. This is possible only in the network marketing business. I have seen this happening right in front of my eyes during the last 20 years.

On the contrary, many people start this business and don't succeed. They didn't do enough to succeed in this business. Sometimes, people join this business out of sheer excitement when they see successful leaders up on the stage, their lifestyle and their recognition. However, they fail to follow the work ethic and commitment these leaders showed while building the business. What people see on the stage is the finished product. They can't learn much from there. What they need to focus on is the quantum of hard work that has gone behind in the making of these leaders.

Let me give you an example here.

When we were growing up as kids, often a street vendor selling flutes used to visit our area. He played melodious tunes of the famous songs from the movies on his flute. Listening to his flute was really a treat to the ears. He had many flutes in his basket to sell. We would buy flutes from him thinking that we will also play good tunes like him.

Reaching home, we would blow the flute but no good music would come out. We tried desperately but all in vain. Then we would throw the flute in some corner of the home and always thought that the flute that vendor was playing was a good one. Probably, he has not given us the right flute. We didn't understand back then. In fact, there's music in the flute but we didn't know how to play that. It needs hard work of learning for weeks and months and a considerable amount of practice before music flows out of the flute. Actually, this is true for any musical instrument.

> **Success has a peculiar phenomenon of leaving behind footprints. Footprints that others can follow to become successful. Success breeds success. When you succeed, your team gets motivated and they want to replicate you. When your team succeeds, you have greater success.**

Unsuccessful people take up Network Marketing Business by seeing the success of leaders on stage. They don't put in the required amount of effort, consistency, learning and routine and give up, like we used to throw away the flute.

> There is always butter in milk but it needs to be churned out.

Over the years, I've seen many people achieving great heights in this business. They succeeded because they duplicated successful people who taught them the cardinal virtues of this business.

There are many stories of rags to riches in this business. I have learnt and noticed some of the virtues that successful people have. I'm sure, when you live these traits and build this business with full integrity and commitment, you'll surely rise big time.

Having Vision, Self-Belief and Foresightedness

Successful people always have a great vision which helps them in building big teams. Vision is not eye-sight. It's about looking ahead and anticipating the future. People having vision always trust their instincts and they've tremendous self-belief. They know what they're doing and why they're doing so.

They outline guidelines for their teams and help them achieve their goals. They've foresightedness and can anticipate how big the team is going to be in the future. Based on that, they chalk out their programs and strategies. Successful leaders always think in advance and set advanced goals.

They're hungry people

When I was new to the business, I listened to many successful people building the business in matured markets such as the US, Canada, Japan, Malaysia and Australia. Their wisdom and knowledge helped me immensely to understand nuggets of the business at an infancy stage.

I learnt that one should always look for hungry people to build this business and not the sharpest one. They taught me that hungry person will certainly overtake the sharpest guy building this business. Here, hungry doesn't mean hungry for food; it means hungry for success. I learnt that hard work will always beat talent when talent does not work hard. Successful networkers have always been hungry for success.

Consistent and Persistent Efforts

Successful people in Network Marketing always make consistent and persistent efforts. While being consistent means doing something daily or regularly but not many people understand the word persistent. Persistent means putting in the same effort again and again despite receiving adverse results.

> When the going gets tough, the tough gets going. Only those who stay persistent get the desired results.

I always ask my team a question, "What is stronger, a drop of water or a stone?"

Obviously, a stone is stronger than a drop of water in the physical sense. However, when the same drop of water consistently drops on the stone for a longer period of time, it creates a crater on the stone. The power isn't in the drop of water. The power is in its consistency to hit the same point again and again.

Successful people always display immense courage and despite facing rejections, they always commit themselves to action. That's the hallmark of their success.

Master in Relationship Building

This is one of the most important traits of a successful leader in Network Marketing. They are masters in building and maintaining relationships and rapport with their team members.

Leaders connect quickly with their audience and keep them engaged. They always put the focus on others and have an eye to eye contact. They are non-judgemental and always refrain themselves from making or passing judgements about people.

These leaders are active listeners and show genuine interest in listening to people. They always display great skills in listening by being absolutely present there at that point in time.

Extra-mile Mentality

Successful people have the habit of going the extra-mile and stretching themselves beyond their limits. It creates a definiteness of purpose and they don't wait for things to happen; they simply do what they need to do. They're proactive in their work ethic.

When people do more than of what they're required to do and they do it with full commitment and generosity, it's very satisfying and uplifting. They become role-models for others to emulate. This habit of successful people differentiates them from the masses.

Inspiring and Motivating

While building teams, successful people always keep the team members engaged and inspire them to grow. Inspiration is something which gets new people started and motivation is something which keeps them going.

Great leaders are always great influencers. The team feels involved and raring to go. The basic difference between a crowd and a team is that of leadership and direction. The leader is always motivating the team first by doing it personally and then letting them grow in a conducive environment.

Never Give-up Attitude

Leaders who have built a successful Network Marketing Business have an attitude of never giving up. They never give up on their dreams and goals and are always ready to help their teams achieve their goals. No matter what the situation they may be in, you will always find them smiling, encouraging and motivating.

This is a very important trait of great leaders. They act as catalysts to enhance the performance of their teams in difficult situations. They lead from the front. Their courage and determination lift the team up to perform.

Great Communicator and Coach

When you closely watch successful leaders in Network Marketing, you see a sense of calmness prevailing on their faces and they are always happy. They are great communicators to their teams and know exactly how to drive the team forward in achieving their target.

The ease and effectiveness with which they communicate is really commendable and a matter of great learning for the team. They know their subject very well and understand what the team needs. Impeccable speech and immaculate body language make these leaders wonderful business coaches.

They are great duplicators

Duplication is the key to success in Network Marketing. You don't have to reinvent the wheel. Successful leaders master the art of duplication. They believe in the formula of Learn, Teach and Duplicate. They're the master trainers who train the trainers. That's why they create such huge organizations in the business.

Duplication creates the multiplier effect and because of it, the teams grow exponentially. Your success in Network Marketing business is directly proportional to the number of leaders that you duplicate. Successful leaders create a big trail of duplicators in their team to leverage the benefit of the multiplier.

Magnetic Personality

The process through which these leaders go, they become magnets. Firstly, it's their ability to attract people and secondly, their approachability creates a positive outlook and they become magnetic personalities and their teams follow them unconditionally. The team always believes that they're in the right hands.

When you meet such people, you find them very engaging and you will be surprised to see how quickly they find the mutual point of interest to communicate and deliberate. They create a bond between themselves and the audience and make them feel involved. The best way to become a magnet is to get closely associated with the one who is already a magnet. This is the power of association.

Creative and Innovative

Steve Jobs, the greatest visionary of our times said, "Innovation distinguishes between a leader and a follower."

I've observed that leaders of Network Marketing Business have been innovative and creative in developing their business. They always try to create new techniques and strategies for their teams and innovate new ways for their growth. They come out with different ways to reward and recognize the performance and achievement of the team members.

This creates excitement and a sense of belongingness in the team. These leaders think out of the box to come up with brilliant ideas and lead the teams upfront to turn dreams into reality.

Leaders in this explosion of Social Media and Internet

There are over 3 billion social media users worldwide and the number is increasing every day. To put into perspective, about one-third of the world's total population is using one or other form of social media to communicate. This has great business potential that needs to be tapped. One of the biggest benefits is the sheer number of people that we can interact with and that too without any filter.

Successful leaders are those who adapt to the changes happening around them and use them to grow their business. In the past few years, the advent of Social Media and the Internet has changed the game head-on. Social Media has become an effective and valuable means to reach out to a new set of potential customers and prospects.

It is a wonderful tool to grow your team and build a successful business. Many successful leaders have grown their business to greater heights by using this as an effective tool. This is a big game changer and can trigger major growth in the Network Marketing Business. Here are the key points highlighting how social media can help you as a lead magnet:

- **Faster Communication**
  Social Media has enabled faster and quicker communication. You can use it to communicate with your teams sitting in your home or office as they are just a click away from you. When you post certain information, everyone gets it instantaneously. The important point is that everyone will get the same information at the same time. This makes information reach a greater number of people at a faster pace, authentic and unfiltered.

- **Brand Building**
  With the use of social media tools such as Facebook, Twitter, Instagram and Snapchat, you can create your own personal brand and position yourself in front of your prospective clients. Your brand contains who you're, what you do and stand for, your hobbies, work and interests. Just imagine, you can attract like-minded people across the globe sharing similar beliefs. They can be your potential prospects and help you in list building.

- **Expand the Reach**
  With Social Media, the territory is not a restriction any longer. With just a click, you can reach out to millions of users around the world. This can help you build a prospective list of clients in a particular area that you wish to visit in the near future and thus your business can go to different places where you had no previous contacts. You can have a global business by using social media applications and tools.

- **Strengthening Bonds**
  There are many tools available in social media that let you interact with your teams throughout the world. By using these applications and tools, you stay connected with your team and keep their morale high. They also feel privileged that you are personally investing your time in them for their growth. This strengthens the bond with them and there are fewer chances of people quitting. You're always updated on the developments in your team.

  It facilitates connection and maintains the relationship. When you personally go there in future, there is a well-established bond which is already there with your team with the support of social media.

- **Attraction and Curiosity Approach**
  Like in the conventional style of approaching people by igniting their curiosity, you can use social media to create your profile and pose some qualifying questions to check the interest of the person on the other side. This can be a good lead generation idea. If the person on the other side is interested in your profile, you can communicate with him/her and propose your business.

- **Conducting Webinar and YouTube Content**
  Webinars are a wonderful leveraging tool that can be used to do business presentations. Many successful leaders in Network Marketing are using this application to reach their audience and share the business plan with them. Similarly, creating video presentation about products, training and business plans on YouTube can

help your teams use them as per their convenience and use it as a tool to grow their business.

I've seen many successful leaders putting a lot of content on YouTube and other platforms to facilitate their teams about products and leadership.

Why Do People Fail in Network Marketing?

When I tell people about how great this business is, a few of them ask me a question. If this is such a great business then why do people fail in Network Marketing Business?

My answer is upfront. People fail in any business so why so much emphasis only on this business?

This is because we share this business with others. We can offer our business to others. They can't do that.

In traditional business, no one shares the secrets of the business with others. We tell others everything about this business. The biggest secret of this business is that there's no secret. It's an open book. Since this is something unique to them, they become sceptical.

Having built this business successfully, in the last 20 years, I have met thousands of people, visited so many families and shared the business with so many people. Not everyone joined my business and also not everyone who joined my business succeeded. I know why people fail and succeed in Network Marketing. A student who has failed in the examination can't tell why he failed. Had he known why he failed; he would have passed. It is only a teacher who knows exactly why the student failed in the exam. Let me give you a clue.

You meet people who have failed in Network Marketing Business, ask them what they did. Write it down. Do exactly what they did for two years and I can guarantee that you will also fail. On the other side, you meet successful people in this business, ask them what they did. Write it down. Do exactly what they did for two years and I can guarantee that you will also succeed.

> Simple things are easy to do but at the same time, they're easy not to do as well. It requires self-discipline.

For example, how many of us know that morning walk is good for health?

How many actually go for a morning walk every day?

It is that simple. Network Marketing Business is a simple business with a rewarding career but still, people don't succeed in it. People fail to do simple things in this business and fail because of a lack of consistency. They simply don't comprehend the simplicity of this business.

People don't plan to fail; they fail to plan. No one who gets into this business joined the business to fail, it's only that they could not succeed. Success needs discipline, success needs commitment, success needs consistent and persistent efforts, success needs motivation and above all, success needs hunger.

> Success is 1% Inspiration and 99% Perspiration. Success needs the perseverance to stay on course despite facing challenges. It is the process of overcoming.

After carefully scrutinizing the people who could not succeed in this business, there're a few traits that are common to all those who failed. I'm listing them below for you. The idea to pen it down for you is to alert you. Avoid these habits and build a successful business to achieve your goals and inspire others.

Common Traits of people who failed in Network Marketing Business

1. Lack of vision
2. No clear dreams and goals
3. Lack of burning desire or emotional dream
4. Lack of work ethic and discipline
5. Habit of procrastination
6. Unwillingness to invest time and money
7. Not willing to learn and listen
8. Fear of rejection and failure
9. Always making excuses
10. Fault finding attitude rather than fact-finding

I've deliberately not explained the traits of the unsuccessful people because that does not serve the purpose of this book. The purpose of writing the book is to help you achieve success in network marketing. Now you know the traits of both successful and unsuccessful people in the Network Marketing Business. You need to figure out where and with whom you want to stand. I prefer to stand with the winners.

➢ I always remember the mantra by Vince Lombardi, a famous American Football Coach, "Winners never quit and quitters never win."

Just to recapitulate....

- ➲ Success is a planned event and never by chance; it's always by choice. The beauty of Network Marketing Business is that your success triggers your team to succeed. They can follow the path that you have created. Success always leaves behind footprints for others to emulate.

- ➲ If you want to learn from a leader, follow the process which led them to success. The process has all the elements that you can follow and become successful.

- ➲ You should be hungry for success. Identify the leader you want to follow. Great leaders inspire others to succeed.

- ➲ Foresightedness, consistent and persistent efforts, relationship building, motivation and great communication skills are some of the hallmarks of great leaders. They never give up, despite facing challenges.

- ➲ Social media and the internet are the biggest game-changers for the Network Marketing Business. They have accelerated growth of such businesses in India. They can help you become a lead magnet and facilitate faster communication and brand building by strengthening bonds and expanding your reach.

- ➲ Success is the process of overcoming the obstacles. Only those who stay on course, despite facing challenges always succeed. Many people fail in Network Marketing Business because they do not withstand challenges and quit. They lack vision and do not have dreams and goals.

- ➲ You become successful only by following the successful leaders. Never let anybody steal your dreams. Winners never quit and quitters never win.

Scribble your Notes

PART II

Identify your WHY

CHAPTER 4

Power of Dreams

Never give up on what you really
want to do. The person with big
dreams is always more powerful
than one with all the facts.

-ALBERT EINSTEIN

Having a Dream

It all starts with a dream. As rightly put out by Eleanor Roosevelt, "The future belongs to those who believe in the beauty of their dreams."

Having a worthwhile dream is the most vital step in your journey towards success. Once you know why you want to do something, you need to identify what are your dreams that you want to fulfil to bring a sense of satisfaction for yourself and motivation for people around you.

People work in their lives predominantly for two reasons. Either they work 'Out of Fear' or 'For a Dream'. Anyone who has some basic knowledge of psychology will understand that Fear is negative and dream is positive. When you have a dream, your steps are positive and are in the right direction.

➤ Having a dream is an essential and valuable asset. Dreams are the driving force and propel us to move forward towards their fulfilment. Dreams motivate us, energize us and refuel us with energy.

People have, over the years, become skeptical about having a dream. They've been discouraged by their peers. They've forgotten to dream because of fear and disappointment. They fear rejection and mockery in case they miss their dreams; that's why they're reluctant to discuss and declare their dreams with their near ones. Even if they've some dream, they keep it to themselves. They limit themselves and settle for less. By doing so, they don't even get what they settled for.

You need to increase the circle of your dreams. People often reduce the circle of their dreams according to the circle of their incomes. Increase the circle of income so that all your dreams can be fulfilled.

Dreams make you stretch beyond your limits. In the crowd of non-dreamers, it is apparently difficult to stick your neck out and declare that you have a dream; here comes the importance of association. That's why there's an old saying, "A man is known by the company he keeps." Nobody asks for your dreams in the job. It's only in the business that people ask what your dreams are.

It's not that all people don't have dreams. Sometimes they've a vague idea. You need to be sure about your dream. There are some elements attached to it which you must understand.

- Is it a worthwhile dream or just a wish?
- Are you serious to achieve it, come what may?
- What are you willing to postpone or give up to achieve that dream?
- What will happen if you don't achieve it?
- Do people around you know about your dream?
- Do you have a game plan in place to achieve your dream?

These are some serious questions that you need to look answers for, not for others but for yourself.

People are so busy in their lives and the moment someone asks them, "Do you have a dream?" They are like "what?" As if this is an out of syllabus question that they need to answer in the examination.

My advice is that you should dream big and for long. Don't let circumstances and situations overpower your dream. You stay steady and set yourself a goal, a target. There're millions of people worldwide who have achieved what they desired for. You can do it too. Don't get disheartened. Many people give up too soon. The moment they find themselves on a difficult wicket, they surrender.

The only one who can hold you back from achieving your dream is you. Your dream should be big enough. If your dreams don't scare you, then probably you haven't got big dreams. You should be very passionate to achieve your dreams. Passion is the fuel which drives a dream further.

Going by my experience of past 20 years in the business of Network Marketing, I have come across many people doing this business, but it is not clear to them why they're doing it; forget about a new person just entering the business. When I'm making that statement, it's not necessarily pejorative. Knowing why to do a thing is the most important and the first step of doing anything.

'Why' is the purpose that drives an Individual to act even when odds are against and chips are down. When you know why you are doing something, it sets you apart from others. Your 'why' motivates and inspires you to take action and achieve your goal. Nothing worthwhile is ever achieved if a person is not clear about why he/she is doing something.

Important to know your 'why'

The word 'WHY' is one amongst the few words in the English language not having a vowel. Nonetheless, its meaning and importance are quite significant and paramount. It is connected with your dream, your reason. This small word has created and written history for many nations. When people have got their 'why', they eventually figure out how to accomplish the task, no matter how big it may be.

When I start showing my presentation to the audience, I begin by writing three words on the board: WHY, WHAT and HOW. This broadly defines the course of my whole presentation. Every time when I do an assessment of the time spent on explaining these three words in the context of my presentation, I have always found out that the maximum time went in the kitty of explaining WHY.

In Network Marketing Business, when people are new, they're not very sure of why they want to build the business. People normally spend less time thinking about why they want to do something whereas it is critically important to know. You need clinical accuracy in identifying the purpose for which you want to build the network marketing business. Else, it will all be futile efforts.

➤ It is always true that a smaller number of people know their 'why', more people know 'how' and most people know 'what' to do.

Let us understand this with the concept of the Golden Circle and learn more about 'why'.

The concept of Golden Circle has been used by world famous writer **Simon Sinek in his book 'Find your Why'.**

The Science of Golden Circle

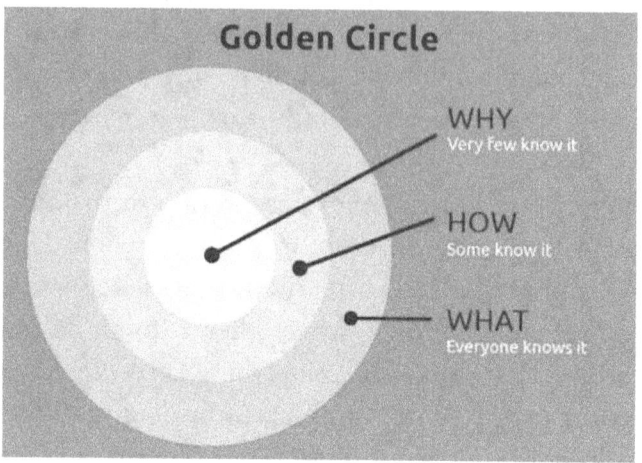

I learnt the concept of Golden Circle while studying Golden Ratios in Mathematics and since then I've seen that it has been used significantly in various other fields too. Golden circle helps us in predicting human behaviour to understand why we do what we do. It provides the clinching fact of how much more we can achieve if we make ourselves aware to start everything we do by first asking 'why'. While many of us know what we are doing and there are many skilful people who know how to do something, there are only a handful of people who can clearly articulate why are we doing that.

Motivation and inspiration fail to keep someone up when the going gets tough and this is the stage when most people quit. Not everyone who starts would finish what they set out to do. The handful of people who make it to the finishing line are those who are clear on why they started in the first place.

Simon Sinek has provided a simple format to construct 'why' statement in his book. You can use this template to create your own 'Why' statement.

TO_____SO THAT_____.

The first blank represents your contribution towards people and the second blank represents the impact of your contribution.

My 'why' statement is:

> *"To train, educate and empower people all over the world so that they can achieve what they desire and thereby improve their lives."*

Your 'why' statement is the most effective tool by which you can communicate your 'why' to yourself and the world. Your 'why' statement should be

- Clear, precise and simple to understand and communicate
- Should show concrete action on your part
- Directed to focus on how will you contribute to others
- Expressed in affirmative language that aptly resonates with you.

In Network Marketing Business, 'why' plays a pivotal role. If your 'why' is clear, 'how' becomes insignificant. That you will figure out somehow. In fact, 'why' is 99% of this business and 'how' is just 1%.

In the Industrial Age, few people knew why to do a thing. Like Henry Ford. He knew why he wanted to start an

Automobile Company that would eventually create history, but he did not know how to run the machines in the factory. On the other hand, some people knew that new machines are being innovated to run in the factories. They learnt the skills to run those machines in anticipation that the factory would hire them. The Industrial Age gave birth to jobs and people started learning the 'know-how' for people who knew the 'know-why'.

> ➤ "People who know why to do a thing always employ people who know how to do that thing."

In the Information Age, 'why' signifies your dreams, goals, target and mission. That is why you will see a few leaders who motivate and inspire people and create that magic influence that separates them from the rest of the people. Even if they know nothing about the Golden Circle, I'm sure it occurs naturally to them through their wisdom.

When I meet my new team players who have recently joined my organization, the first question I ask them after starting an initial discussion is why they joined the business. In the beginning, when they are new, they've a vague idea about 'why' and not at all specific. It's not unusual and strange rather obvious. Sometimes, they come out with readymade statements heard from others during the presentation. I become very patient with them because, during my initial days in the business, even I didn't have a clear idea about why I was doing the business then.

> Many people join this business not because they've understood the business but only because you are doing it.

'Why' is not the first choice of the people; it needs to sink in. However, it's very important to bring clarity to it. 'Why' needs to be dissected further. The main job of the leader is to deal with the new persons in helping them dissect 'why' down to clinical precision. It's where counselling plays a vital role.

When you are new to this business, take help of your leaders to initiate and induct a new person in the business. Make use of different forums to introduce new people to your leaders. Your leaders will identify sharp persons. Once these people have been identified, you should book an appointment with your leader for their home visit and let your leader begin doing the basic things with them. While he is busy doing all the basic things with the new person, you need to watch him closely. It's your learning time.

> People may not get in the business knowing what you do, but they join your business knowing why you do what you do.

All over the world, people join Network Marketing Business because they want to achieve something they couldn't achieve in their current profession. That something is Dream. Maybe it's more money, vacations, time for family, buying a luxury house or/and a car or anything else. The dream is the driving force in this business. There is no boss of yours in this business. You're your own boss. Now, that's good as well as bad news.

When you have a dream about which you are passionate and you want to make that dream a reality, nobody can stop you. In the absence of a dream, you will struggle in this business. After a day of hectic work in the office, what will inspire you to go out, meet people, show presentations and build networks other than having a dream? The more the merrier. There is no restriction that you can have one dream at a time. You can have as many as you want. This business has got the potential to fulfil all your dreams. The only thing is that you need to commit yourself to this business.

> **Don't let circumstances and situations overpower your dream. You stay steady and set yourself a goal, a target. There are millions of people worldwide who have achieved what they desired. You can do it too. Don't get disheartened. Many people give up too soon. The moment they find themselves on a difficult wicket, they surrender.**

Making your Dream more realistic

It's good to have certain dreams in your mind, but you need to bring them in front of your eyes as well. So, the first thing is that you write down your dreams. Yes, your brain will try to stop you from doing that and ridicule it, still, you need to persist and write down your dreams on a paper.

There is power and magic when you write down your dreams. Dreams give birth to thoughts and thoughts turn into action which thereby brings out desired results. You need to understand this process. The mind is already there, it's only thoughts that are imported into the mind. Hence, your mind manifests your thoughts.

The state of the mind determines the thoughts. You can't have positive thoughts if your mind is surrounded by negative environment unless you're a sage. That's why we say 'association' is important. A positive association creates an ambiance wherein the mind feels relaxed and then comes the positive thoughts. Make a deliberate attempt to be in the positive association.

> Learn to switch on and switch off your mind.

Your logical mind will not let you do the things which haven't been taught to you or happened with you before. Let me give you a clue for your emotional mind to understand.

You must have seen that when a lady is expecting a baby, the family pastes beautiful pictures of cute babies on the walls of her room. Why is it so? Because when she looks at those pictures, her brain processes the pictures and sends signals in the forms of thoughts. She starts thinking that she will also have a cute baby like in those pictures.

Another example is that of gym trainers putting big posters of great bodybuilders on the walls of the gym. They do so that the clients who want to build muscles can look at those pictures and start believing that one day they too will have great muscles like those bodybuilders.

Dream Board or Vision Board

A Dream Board is a collection of pictures of your dreams. It's a great way to bring a more concrete and realistic feeling to your dreams. It's a visual tool that keeps you motivated and uplifts you when the going gets tough. It is believed that when you have your dream board right in front of your eyes, it activates the Law of Attraction to bring desired results into your life. You invoke the powers of the universe which help you in achieving all those dreams. Therefore, dream chart or vision board is a very effective tool in your hand towards the fulfilment of your dreams.

Making a dream board is an interesting and fascinating task. You should make your dream board with full vigour, excitement and belief.

Our mind understands pictures better and once you paste pictures of your dream, your brain comprehends and processes it pretty fast. You can find lots of sample images of dream charts online. You can look at those samples and make your own dream board. Pictures create magic in your brain and it is an extremely powerful tool in the realization of your dreams. Visualization has great power. There is power in having dream and visualising them. It gives direction to your thoughts and feelings. It's a scientifically proven fact.

How to Make a Dream Board

You can collect pictures of your dreams and decorate on a chart paper. Paste the chart on the dream board and put it on the wall of your house. It will inspire and motivate you to pursue your dream. Buy a dream board or a vision board from the market. Collect magazines on tours and travels, dress and design, motor cars and all other relevant stuff to your dreams. You can cut pictures from magazines and paste them.

For example, if your dream is to go on a vacation to a beach, cut pictures from the travel magazines or download them from the internet and paste them in on your dream chart. Similarly, you may do it for the car that you like and so on. Involve your family and their dreams in your dream board. It enhances their participation in helping you achieve your dreams. Place your dream board at a prominent place in your home where you are going to see it quite often. There is magic in doing that.

It's possible that someday you have a bad outing and none of your prospects got into the business; back home when you look at your dream board, it will re-energize you. The dream board is also known as the vision board. It's the best tool for using the power of visualization. There have been countless stories on how people achieved everything that they pasted on the dream board.

Network Marketing Business for dreamers. This isn't the business which you are doing under some compulsion. It's neither done under any kind of obligation. People join this business for their dreams and achieve significant milestones in their lives. When they achieve those milestones, they become influencers and motivators for many to follow. Great Networkers share their experiences of how they felt when their dreams materialised into reality.

Freedom is worth it. It's a wonderful sense of achievement. We, in Network Marketing Buisness, not only show dreams to people, but also help them achieve those dreams. We feel happy in their accomplishment and enjoy the celebrations. We are there with them from the beginning, during the process and guiding them in their journey to success.

Once you have identified your 'why' and your dreams are clear to you, it's a positive start. You've started your journey towards success. You've separated yourself from the crowd.

It's a step in the right direction. You should congratulate yourself for taking the baby steps that many are unwilling to take. Don't let anyone steal your dreams. Follow your heart, no matter what happens. The next step is to convert dreams into goals. In the next chapter, you will learn how to set goals and other important aspects associated with it.

Just to recapitulate....

- Know-why is more important than know-how. When your 'why' is clear, 'how' becomes insignificant. Many people know how to do a thing as compared to only a few who know why they want to do something.

- Construct your why statement by using the format

  TO_____SO THAT_____.

  The first blank represents your contribution towards people and the second blank represents the impact of your contribution.

- People may not get in the business knowing what you do, but they join your business knowing why you do what you do.

- You should dream big and long. The dream is the driving force. When dream is big enough, facts don't count. Network Marketing business helps in realizing your dream into reality. Just believe in the power of the system and follow the successful leaders.

- The dream board is an important tool and acts as a reminder. It refuels energy in you when you have a bad day.

- Stay on course when facing situations and challenges. All the people who became successful, found success next door to failure. You need to have the courage and strength to keep on knocking the door. Failure is part of the game.

Scribble your Notes

CHAPTER 5

Goals

> If you want to live a happy life, tie
> it to a goal. Not to people or things.
>
> -**ALBERT EINSTEIN**

Just create a picture in your mind of a football stadium where the world's two best teams are fighting for the world championship. What an electrifying scenario! Eleven best footballers from each team enter the field to take positions. Both the captains reach the centre to kick-start the game. The whole stadium is packed with spectators backing their respective teams. There is excitement in the air. The referee is all set to blow the whistle for the start of the game.

Suddenly, everyone notices that there are no goalposts on the ground on either side. Now, everyone in the stadium is perplexed. What for these 22 players with a football in their feet play if there are no goalposts? What for have the spectators come to the stadium? Will you even call it a football game? **No Goalposts!**

This is just an example of a blunder that supposedly will never happen in a football match. But what about your life? Are you committing that blunder?

How serious this mistake can be? No Goals in life?

You need to think about it on an urgent basis. The first condition for winning any game is that you should be in the game. You can't win the game by sitting there in the spectators' gallery. There, you're merely a spectator. The second condition is that you must know the rules of the game that you're playing. You can't apply rules of cricket in the game of hockey. Learn the rules of the game. Then comes the third condition that you play to your potential.

Some people play the game without having adequate knowledge of the rules by just sitting there in the audience. Nobody is listening and paying attention to what you're saying there.

Same is true for your life. If you want to succeed, get into the game, learn the rules and start playing. The journey begins by setting the goals.

What's that for which you're fighting the game? Let's study **GOALS.**

What are Goals?

Goal = Dream + Date + Measured, Actionable Game Plan

When you've a dream that you want to achieve within a fixed period of time and you're ready to take concrete and measured actions towards it, then it becomes a goal. Goals are specific and quantifiable close-ended dreams with a fixed time frame allocated for achieving them. It's a dream with specific attention and work ethic to be accomplished within a fixed period of time.

Probability of the achievement of your goals is directly proportional to your efforts. Two persons can have the same dream, their goals can be different towards the fulfilment of those dreams. Since goals are quantifiable, they can be broken down into smaller units according to time frame.

SMART Goals

SMART means Specific, Measurable, Attainable, Relevant and Time-Bound.

SMART also means Significant, Meaningful, Action-Oriented, Rewarding and Trackable

You need to set SMART goals to accelerate your performance. Goals are performance accelerators.

How do you feel when somebody gives you a compliment? Do you feel good? Yes, everyone likes to get compliments. That's the reward to the brain. When your brain has processed your dreams, it sends signals in the universe to realise those dreams.

When you set a game plan to achieve those dreams, the powers of the universe guide and help you to achieve them. This has happened for many on this earth and it can work for you too.

Classification of Goals

Based on your dreams, you need to categorize your goals into three parts and put in massive action to achieve them.

1. **Short-Term Goals**
   Goals which you're likely to achieve in less than a years' time are short-term goals. These are the goals which are comparatively easy and fast to be achieved and command less monetary value. Once these goals are achieved, your mind and body start believing in the power of dreams and goals. Your brain feels rewarded.

2. **Medium-Term Goals**
   Goals which can be achieved in 2-3 years' time are medium-term goals. Examples can be buying a car, going on an international vacation, etc.

3. **Long-Term Goals**
   Goals which take 3-5 years to achieve are termed as long-term goals like owning a house, buying a luxury car, etc.

➢ Set a goal in life and then look towards your feet; if they're moving in the direction where your goal is, you'll definitely reach there.

Why do we need to set Goals?

Let's begin this by taking an example.

A person goes to the reservation counter at a Railway Station to book a rail ticket. When he reaches the ticket window, the first thing the booking attendant will ask him is where does he want to go.

Now, if the person is not sure where he wants to go, will he get the ticket? If he says anywhere, will the attendant give him the ticket? No. So the first thing he needs to clarify is where he wants to go. Next, let us assume that he wants to go to Mumbai. The subsequent question would be when do you want to go? Now the person needs to answer this question as well else how would he get the ticket? He cannot say that give me a ticket for any day. That does not make sense. He needs to be sure of the answers to these questions. After that subsequent questions will prop up as to which class, he wants to travel in, etc.

Now the person in the above example has the dream of travelling but he is not clear about the rest of the things.

Similarly, in real life, many people have dreams but they don't have goals and a game plan to bring those dreams into reality. When a simple railway ticket cannot be purchased without certain targeted answers, how do you think you can reach in life where you want to reach without having clear goals?

Would you ever work for a company that has no specific goals and mission statement? Obviously not.

Here comes the importance of why we need to set goals.

1. **Well begun is half done**

   How many times have we heard this statement? What do we mean by well begun? When you have a goal in place, half your work is done. Many people never reach up to this point. They never set a goal. That's why those who do, they're miles ahead. I hope now you understand it better.

People don't set goals in life and even if they do, they are more generic and vaguer like happiness, good health, wealth, social acceptance and successful relationship. Most people don't reach there because the goals were not set properly in the first place.

You need to be specific and precise while setting goals.

2. **Goals give you direction**

   Without a goal, the dream is a scalar quantity having only magnitude and no direction. Goals give you direction. So, you've both direction and magnitude. Achieving something without setting goals and measured action can be sheer luck and you can be called lucky, but with goals and action plan, you're sure to succeed and you'll be called successful.

   When you have goals in place and you are ready to move, it's like you have the navigation system of your car set on the destination where you want to go, now it will tell you to move in the direction which leads to your destination.

3. **Force Multiplier**

   When you have a clearly defined goal and a roadmap ahead, it acts as a force multiplier wherein you will be able to accomplish your goal despite facing challenges. In fact, you will not see the obstacles on the way. Obstacles are something that you see when you take your eyes off the goal. Goals are written down guidelines for the fulfilment of a dream.

4. Goals help in channelizing your energy
    Without goals, you are wanderers like free radicals,
    making other atoms unstable. When you've a goal in
    place, your energy flows in a channel and it becomes
    easy for you to march forward in an organized way.
    There's no chaos and you bring the best out of you.

Top-level athletes of any game, businessmen and top
achievers in their respective fields, all set their goals. It gives
them direction, motivation, vision and game plan going
forward. You need to set your goals. By setting SMART
goals, you can measure your progress and take pride in
their accomplishment. When you meet your goals, you
leverage your time and resources and you'll observe a sense
of achievement, which otherwise looked a tedious grind.

Goal Setting in Network Marketing Business

In the Network Marketing Business, you're your own
boos. You work here for fulfilling dreams and goals which
otherwise remained unfulfilled. So, it is highly incumbent
on you to set goals. It's for you and your team. When you
achieve your goals, you set the ball rolling.

I feel happy to see people who have learnt the skills of
goal setting, set their goals, work towards their realization,
and finally achieve them. I see a sense of joy and fulfilment
on their faces. I feel satisfied to see the whole family happy
when they achieve goals. It refuels and reenergizes them to
set higher goals because they've tasted success. This's the
beauty of this business. Success breeds success and it's very
contagious.

My experience in this industry has made me master the
skills of goal setting and I have spoken on this topic at

various forums. I had the privilege of being invited by other industries and corporate houses to speak on this. I have *read* intensively on this subject and applied it on myself and thousands of my teammates and clients.

I've achieved many goals that I had set for myself and I keep on setting new goals. Even while writing this book, I had set certain writing goals and the outcome of that is in the form of this book, which is in your hands.

You need to understand that it's imperative for all businesses to set goals and when we talk about Network Marketing, it's even more important. My experience says this is the point where most of the networkers falter. For your benefit, I'm going to dwell upon this a little bit in detail. You need to go through this and use it as a reference time and again. Let's revisit the equation that I wrote at the beginning of this chapter.

Goal = Dream + Date + Measured, Actionable Game Plan

You need to understand each component of this equation minutely. It starts with Dream. Make sure you did all the things that I wrote in the previous chapter on Power of Dreams. You need to have a dream and make a dream chart of all your dreams. You need to have dreams in front of your eyes. There is power and magic in writing dreams.

Once you have your dreams in front of your eyes, the next step is when do you want to accomplish those dreams. Depending upon the incomes that you make at different levels in this business, you need to figure when your dreams can become a reality. The third component is Measured and Actionable Game Plan.

You need to sit down with your growing upline and chalk out a roadmap of actions that you need to take so that you can achieve those dreams. When your upline guides you for the actions that you need to take in terms of the number of contacts, meetings, tools-flow, function numbers etc., you need to work on all these immaculately. Break down the action needed to be done into a daily work schedule.

> When you meet your daily goal, you never miss your monthly or yearly goals. That's the magic mantra. Counselling has a very important role to play in Goal Setting.

I've seen many people in Network Marketing who have failed and didn't grow in the business. They think they're doing everything correctly but that is not true. My advice to all those who get stuck in one place in the business is to go back to the basics. Back to the basics is the only way out to get back on track.

Many people set goals but don't achieve them and miss the goal. There is nothing wrong with missing the goals. It is not a crime at all. Even I have missed many times. Many successful leaders have missed their goals. We analyse and check where the deviation in the action is. Then we reset our action.

The problem is always in insufficient action. All you need to check is whether your basics are correct or not. Have you made a game plan for achieving those dreams? Is your daily routine taking you one step forward or not? You need to check the component of Measured, Actionable Game Plan. The problem lies here and the solution lies with you. You need to set your priorities right and put those actions into motion which will help you meet your goals.

> ➤ Set goals in life and ride the vehicle called 'Persistency' and never deboard it till you reach your destination.

Goal Sheet

Once you have broadly set your goals in due consultation and counselling with your growing upline, you need to make a Goal Sheet. A Goal Sheet is an organized way of detailing your goals so that they look presentable and professional. It will help you to demonstrate your goals to your teams to motivate and inspire them. It enables you to declare your goals to yourself and letting people around you know your goals. You can have daily, weekly, monthly and yearly goal sheets depending upon your needs. Prepare a good goal sheet for your goals.

> Many people set goals but don't achieve them. There is nothing wrong with missing the goals. It is not a crime at all. Even I have missed many times. Many successful leaders have missed their goals. We analyse and check where the deviation in the action is. Then we reset our action. The problem is always in insufficient action.

When we speak out our goals to ourselves, there is great power in the spoken goals. Always speak what you want and not what you have or don't want. By speaking your goals, you send signals to the subconscious mind and the universe. There are different formats of goal sheets available online. Select one according to your need and use it for yourself and your team.

Self-Talk

I always begin my Training Session with this statement:

Thank you, God, today is a great day.

Then, I ask my audience and check by a show of hands as to how many of them believe in this and why. I give my perspective of the opening statement. Thank you, God, for giving us a new day and thank you that we could see the light of the day. There are millions of reasons every day for which we can thank God.

I always teach people that if you want to change the way you live, you need to do two things. One, change the way you think and two, change the way you speak. These two changes can make your life a dream life. I conduct webinars and workshops on my specially designed program **"TRAIN YOUR BRAIN"** in which I coach people to think in the way which can benefit them in their business, relationships, profession, health and various other aspects of life.

I train athletes to program their minds towards winning. I have designed a special program for students under "TRAIN YOUR BRAIN" to help them overcome fear and anxiety of Examinations and bring the best out of them. In the Network Marketing business, I have trained thousands of business owners and helped them achieve success in achieving their goals by using techniques taught through this program.

Thinking and speaking affect our lives more than anything else. Self-talk is an effective technique of speaking to yourself and the universe. It's a deliberate attempt to feed your brain with positive things and train your brain to think and act in a particular way. It's fodder to the brain.

Feeding Neck Up

The human mind is constantly speaking to itself through thoughts which constantly go through mind all the time. A man is nothing but the outcome of his thoughts oscillating in his mind and consistently sending signals. If these thoughts are channelized in a positive way, the results are astonishing.

While every day, we eat food at least three times a day feeding our body neck down, we starve our body Neck Up. Now, if a piece of land is left unattended, weeds grow up automatically. Growing some crop on it is a deliberate attempt and for that, we cultivate the land, put seeds into it, add fodder and water it regularly. Same is our mind. We need to feed our body Neck Up to bring out desired results.

In Network Marketing Business, Self-Talk helps in feeding the mind. Your goal sheet contains your goals to be achieved over a period of time. Speak those goals to yourself as if you've already achieved them. By doing that consistently you're programming your mind. The mind starts believing in them and then you back them up with action. If you follow these steps, you will see miracles happening in your business and life.

Let's understand how to construct positive self-talk. This template will help you formulate your own self-talk. You need to write down your self-talk and make deliberate attempts to speak out to your mind. You may even stand in front of the mirror and speak. Look straight into your eyes in the mirror and do the self-talk. It's a proven and tested technique.

Let's say one of your goals is to shed 10 kg weight in six months. Even before figuring out how to do it, first start speaking it.

The template is

Thank You, God, _____by _____.

While the first blank is the outcome you want to achieve, the second blank is a definite deadline by which you want to achieve that goal.

Now, since in this scenario, your goal is to shed 10 kg weight in six months, you calculate when six months are over, get that date and construct your statement.

> *Thank you, God, I have shed 10 kg weight by 31st March 2020.*

Now, the first part is the gratitude by thanking God, second is the desired outcome as if it has already happened and the third part is the date by which you wish to achieve that goal.

By using this template, you can create your self-talk statements and start speaking to yourself.

Initially, your brain will ridicule you; but when you stay persistent, it will start believing. You will start exploring ways of how to achieve those goals. Now, back it up with a measured diet and exercise plan. Remember,

Goal = Dream + Date + Measured, Actionable Game Plan

By feeding your brain neck up, you are creating a positive mindset and your brain will act accordingly. Self-talk will help you in raising your self-image and start believing in yourself before others start believing in you. Research has shown that people who set goals and use this powerful technique of self-talk are more likely to achieve their goals and much faster as well.

I've seen a tremendous amount of success being achieved by millions of people throughout the world by using the powerful combination of Goal-Setting and Self-Talk. This has helped me significantly in achieving the success that I enjoy today. I sincerely thank God for everything that has happened in my life so far and for all that which is going to happen in future. When you use this combination, you'll achieve whatever you desire in life. But don't forget to thank God for everything. Make gratitude a way of life.

Just to recapitulate....

- Setting goals is important in life. Goals are specific and quantifiable close-ended dreams for which you are willing to put forth massive action. Always set SMART goals.

- When you have a goal in place, half your work is done. You need to be specific and precise in setting goals and there needs to be clinical accuracy in determining goals. You get direction when you set goals.

- Goal setting is an important step in the Network Marketing Business and you need to sit with your leaders while doing this exercise.

- There is nothing wrong in missing the goals; it's not a crime. All you need to do is check your actions. Whatever needs to be changed is in your action. Go back to the basics.

- Goal sheet is an effective tool for declaring your goals to yourself and your team. It is a professional and organized way of presenting your goals.

- There is power in speaking your goals. Make use of Self-Talk to reinforce your goals. Self-Talk is a proven technique of speaking to yourself and the universe. It's a deliberate attempt to feed the brain with positive and desirable material. Learn the techniques of creating your own Self-Talk statements. Always show gratitude towards what you have. Make gratitude a way of life.

Scribble your Notes

PART III

What Not to Do

CHAPTER 6

Cardinal Rules

You have to learn the rules of the
game, and then you have to play
better than anyone else.

-ALBERT EINSTEIN

Learning the language of the business

Every business and profession have their own vocabulary, language and rules. While you need to learn and adapt to this vocabulary, there're certain non-negotiable norms and rules which you need to adhere to right from the beginning. The sooner you understand and practise the rules, the faster are your chances of growth in the business.

> ➢ Rules are not negative; they're the safeguard to your survival in the business. Rules let you understand what doesn't work in the business and you needn't waste your time by committing those offences. Rules provide you protection.

Many people think that rules make their lives tough. It's not so. On the contrary, rules make your life safe, secure and simple. You can save yourself against any accident or damage. You're being forbidden to do certain things because by doing those things, you can put yourself in some kind of inconvenience or trouble.

Every business, profession or job has rules to follow. We start following rules from our childhood. They protect us from harm.

You can't claim ignorance towards not knowing the rules. When you learn to drive a car, at the same time you need to follow traffic rules. You can't say that let me first learn how to drive the car after that you will learn the rules. You need to learn the rules even before you start learning driving skills. You can't escape by saying that you were ignorant. Rules are there even if you don't know them.

When you're caught up in a situation, try to get out of there without compromising with the rules. There isn't any point in getting entangled in another situation. Always follow the Japanese philosophy of doing it right the first time. Challenges will come; life will throw challenges at you to check whether you still have that zeal to overcome challenges. Life always rewards to them who overcome. Overcome to become. The process of overcoming rejection is a bit tedious but possible.

Successful people in all walks of life have gone through this process and eventually achieved greater heights. If you're following the same process, you are sure to taste success. Only those who undertake this journey will meet success. No one achieved success without failing and facing challenges.

> When you succeed, you get lot of things such as praise, respect, attention, rewards and awards but no learning because there isn't any in success. On the contrary, when you fail, you will not get all those things but only learning. So, don't get disheartened when you fail. Learn as much as you can. That is your learning time. This is how you will go up on the learning curve.

I've been a student of this business for two decades now and I think two decades is a good enough period to understand what works and what doesn't. I have built huge teams, made many mistakes, but today I'm successful. Mistakes that I committed, have taught me to correct myself and my course of action.

In this chapter, we will deliberate on some of the things that I learnt over this period of time in this business. If you know what you don't need to do, then space is wide open to do all those things which will benefit in building a huge business.

> **Life will throw challenges at you to check whether you still have that zeal to overcome challenges. Life always rewards to them who overcome. Overcome to become. The process of overcoming the rejection is a bit tedious but possible. Successful people in all walks of life have gone through this process and eventually achieved greater heights. If you're following the same process, you are sure to taste success.**

Today, I speak at different forums across many industries as a keynote speaker and also do counselling with a wide spectrum of people from society; be it businessmen, sportsmen, students, and corporates. I teach them through team-building exercises. One thing is common in all those teams. They all make mistakes. When they make mistakes, it means they are progressing higher on the learning curve.

In Network Marketing Business, there are certain rules which you need to follow else you will not succeed here. The higher the business, the more is the need for these rules. Also, it is the experts who are more likely to break the rules.

When someone is learning to drive a car, they will stop way behind the stop line but when one becomes an expert, he/she may try to jump the signal. Mistakes that we make are lessons. In this business, you can commit a new mistake every day but don't repeat the same mistake. This is, in fact, true for any strata of life.

The beauty of Network Marketing business is that here, every day is a new day. You can forget whatever wrong you did yesterday and take a fresh guard today keeping in mind not to repeat the mistake again. This is the business where you may fail more but still come out with flying colours. This luxury is not available to traditional businesses because one wrong decision on a day can have a long-lasting effect on operations and can prove to be fatal.

Words of Caution

Although Network Marketing is a very forgiving business, if you compromise with the rules intentionally, you will be phased out of the business. Since this is a peoples' business and no two people have the same thinking and temperament, you need to be ultra-cautious in dealing with people. While you can rise to fame by your hard work, if some rule is not followed, the same set of people will bring you down in no time. Integrity is the key to success in this business or for that matter in life.

I've seen big businesses collapsing like a pack of cards when certain rules are compromised. I believe you will learn from these mistakes, avoid them and build a big business. That will be my incentive for writing this book. These rules are there because some people broke those rules and lost their teams.

The idea is to alert you beforehand so that you may not repent at a later stage and get disheartened. Let's discuss some of the rules that are important to be taken notice of right from the word go.

1. **Don't tell, show the business**
    Network Marketing Business is about three things – plan, people and products. You share the business plan and products with people. The plan is the most important tool to present your business. You need to show the plan

to the people. Here, the important word is 'show'. Do not tell the plan.

There has to be magic in showing the plan. You need to show the plan with proper posture, good body language and confidence. Your plan and your attitude will draw or withdraw people. So, you need to show the plan with excitement and command. You need to keep your audience engaged.

Become a good presenter in showing your business enthusiastically to your prospects. Remember, people first join you and later they get to know about the company and the products.

2. **Don't talk much**

   Respect the other person's time. Do not talk more than what is required. Your presentation should be short and crisp. Follow the time schedule strictly. You need to put facts and figures of the business in front of the person sitting in front of you. Don't start telling your own life story. People just want to listen to what is for them in the presentation.

   If you are showing the plan in somebody's house, follow the thumb rule of leaving the person's house ten minutes before he wants you to leave. Respect the privacy of others. Don't ask offending questions that can hurt someone. Be sure of what you speak.

3. **Don't complicate, keep it simple**

   Keep your presentation simple. Your presentation should follow a logical and interesting sequence. Don't complicate your plan by using heavy words that send people searching for the dictionary. Simple things are easy to duplicate and you are in the duplication business.

After seeing your presentation, the other person should feel that it is very simple. If he thinks that it is only you who can do that, your plan is not good. He should feel that he can do it easily. Remember, we are in the business of "Learn, Teach and Duplicate". Keep it simple.

4. **Don't ever put down people or their profession**
As I have told you that it's a business of the people, respect their ego. Do not ever put down people or their profession. Respect what they do. For example, you are doing the business, but your prospect may be doing a job, do not put down their job. That will hurt the other person's ego and blow them away.

You need to build rapport with your audience. Why blow of minds by unnecessarily putting down other person's job or profession? Use a smart question-answer method to make your presentation participative without hurting people.

5. **Don't make false and unrealistic promises**
Never make false or unrealistic promises to your audience. You are not in a quick-rich scheme. Show people honest facts and figures. When you show them things that their mind can't accept, they withdraw from the plan. While showing the big picture of your business, you need to understand the composition of your audience.

New people may not digest what you say easily. Don't make unrealistic promises which cannot be achieved. This destroys the faith of the people and they may not join your organization.

6. **Don't ever put down other Companies**
Many companies are offering Network Marketing Business in India. While you have every right to show how great your company is, never ever put down other businesses. It is not good ethics and your audience also does not like this. You just focus on the presentation of your company.

You have no right to downgrade the products and business of other companies doing similar kind of business. Great leaders don't put others down. They uplift and encourage people.

7. **Don't pre-judge people**
You are looking for hungry people for your business. People who are hunting and chasing their dreams. They are the people who will join your business. How will you come to know about this trait in them? Only when you show the plan to them. Do not pre-judge anyone whether he would join the business or not. Let the plan do the magic.

Showing the plan is a filter which will filter the right people for you. So, your job is to just show the plan and let that person take the decision. Sometimes, we start thinking about what the other person would think. Don't encroach on other people's territory. Let them make their own decisions.

8. **Don't re-invent the wheel**
Many people think that they can build this business without learning from successful people. They try to do it in their own way without learning. The chances are that they will not succeed. You have a successful team that is willing to guide you. Just follow them and do what they have done.

I always tell people that there are two ways of doing this business. Either 'My Way' or 'Right Way'. You need to follow the 'Right Way' as your way of doing this business and you will be successful.

9. **Don't sell products unethically**

    In today's age of online marketing, e-commerce and social media, many people try to create short-cuts to succeed in the Network Marketing Business. They follow unethical practices and sell their products online which is against the code of conduct of the company. This violates their business agreement with the company but still, they do it by creating fake identities.

    Online selling is a menace that destroys the spirit of level playing game of this business. Some people offer huge discounts to sell their products through shops just to achieve some level in the business. We need to introspect.

    Is this right way of doing the business? Did we come to this business to do unethical things?

    Can we compromise with our principles? Is it sustainable?

    Because of a handful of people doing it the unethical way, hundreds and thousands of people building this business with integrity get disheartened and discouraged. We should fish out these bad fishes from the pond.

10. **Don't use people for your selfish motives**

    Never ever use people in your team to fulfil your selfish motives; it's teamwork. Don't destroy the fabric of team-spirit. Build a long-lasting business which is going to serve your generations.

Leaders build it right and build it once. Never put people under pressure to achieve certain levels in the business. That is not going to sustain as they will soon understand your motive and leave your team. Leaders always lead by example. You need to set the bar high. Treat people with respect and dignity. Serve people and help them achieve their goals in the right manner.

11. **Check upline first up**

When you are new to this business, you may have your own ideas to build this business. There is nothing wrong in that. But before applying that idea, please take the advice of your growing upline on that. It can save your time and money. It is possible that your uplines may already have tried that idea but failed. They can guide you by their experience. You can make use of their experience and avoid committing the same mistake.

Remember, there is no post-mortem in Network Marketing Business. You need to check before implementing anything new for the first time that has not been taught to you before. This rule is to help you avoid mistakes and save time and money.

12. **No Negative gossips in the business**

There is no room for any negative gossips in this business because anything negative multiplies faster here. It can destroy your teams. Protect your teams from negative news and negative social media propaganda. Negative spreads like fire in the jungle and there is no stopping. So, the best is to avoid it upfront.

If anything negative comes to you from anywhere, don't pass it on further. Be a shock-absorber. Before passing on anything in your team, always check the golden question. Is it going to benefit my team in growing their business further? If the answer is no, then do not forward it.

13. **No Messing up with anyone's spouse, money or ego**
This is the basic fundamental of building teams for long-term. Always build it on right principles and ethics. Respect your teammate's ego. Never mess up with your teammate's money. Give respect to the family members of the team. Never mess up with anyone's spouse. This will obliterate team spirit and values. These are the core values of building the teams and must never be compromised.

14. **Get rid of toxic elements**
If you find anyone messing up with his conduct and destroying the core values of the team, you need to send him off as quickly as possible. Don't let toxic elements destroy the fabric of your team. You need to flush them out before it is too late. If you find someone not following the system, stop lending support there until they mend their way.

15. **No space for arrogance and bossism**
Network Marketing is purely a team game. It's a level playing field for everyone. There is no room to be arrogant. The responsibility is to serve and uplift the people and help them in achieving their desired goals through this business and teach them to duplicate the same further in their teams. Nobody is anybody's boss in this business. All are equal players and like in any sport, there will be seniors and new teammates.

Everyone deserves due respect and commands the same authority. While it is obvious that new team members will give due respect to seniors, that does not mean the seniors are their boss. There is no space for arrogance and bossism while building teams and a long term sustainable and profitable business. Work with your sponsor and work with those you sponsor.

➢ The Network Marketing Concept is growing fast. India market is maturing and there's churning taking place. New companies are coming into the field. New and innovative products are being introduced. You need to stay steady and keep your folks together. Now is the time when leaders will be tested the most.

If you don't build your business with honesty and integrity, no matter how big you become, your business can collapse and teams can switch to a new company or vanish. You need to be very cautious in your approach. People who will build huge businesses in the coming years are now coming forward. India is a young country. There is a Tsunami of Networkers to come. They'll follow the real leaders.

Don't dilute your integrity doing petty things. Never compromise with your principles and ethics. Don't do anything which is not duplicable for a long-term business. You may get short-term success but you will surely loose in the long-run. Rules set the frame within which you need to perform. Once you start living within the rules, life becomes simple and you know exactly what to do and what not to do.

Just to recapitulate....

- Every business and profession have certain rules to be followed. You need to learn the vocabulary of the business as early as possible. Rules make your life simple and easy.

- Not knowing the rules doesn't allow you to break the rule.

- When you learn from mistakes, you go up on the learning curve. Breaking the rules can cause problems. In Network Marketing Business, you have the advantage that you will be taught the rules in advance by your leaders. You just need to adhere to those rules.

- Higher the business, more important are the rules. When rules are compromised, big teams can vanish. So be ethical and honest. Integrity is the key to success in this business.

- Never hurt anybody's ego by putting down their job or profession. Never put down other companies doing Network Marketing Business.

- Never do unethical things in the business, like selling products online and undercutting the price. Never use people for your own selfish motives. There is no scope for arrogance or bossism.

- The Indian market is maturing and churning is taking place. Leaders need to keep their folks together. Do the business ethically.

Scribble your Notes

PART IV

Setting the Foundation Right

CHAPTER 7

Basics to Follow

Successful people master the basics.
They become phenomenal by
consistently doing the little
things well.

-BILLY ALSBROOKS

In the previous chapter, we discussed about the things that you need to avoid in order to save time and money and ensure your survival in the business. In this chapter, we will discuss the things to do in the business. It doesn't matter whether you're new to the business or already there for some time, if you want to grow further in the business, you need to follow the basics.

I remember the commentary of former Yorkshire and England Cricketer Sir Geoffrey Boycott wherein he emphasised that when a player has lost his form, he can only gain it back when he's batting in a match in the middle of crease. He can't get back his lost form in the dressing room, practice session, rather right there on the crease of the match. He always stressed on Back to Basics.

> When from your peak, you hit the rock-bottom; the only way to rise back to your crowning glory is by going back to the basics. Basics are equally important for beginners as well.

Building the basics right

Building a successful Network Marketing Business is similar to laying the foundation for a tall building. Like, the foundation plays a vital role in a structure, in Network Marketing, Basic Steps help in laying the foundation of a solid business. When the foundation is strong, you can build a tall building consisting of several floors, likewise setting the right foundation helps you in building a long-term profitable and sustainable Network Marketing Business.

Setting the right structure is the basic building block of a profitable business. In this chapter, we'll discuss the basic steps that you need to learn and practice. Doing these basic steps over and over again will help you develop a strong and profitable Network Marketing Business.

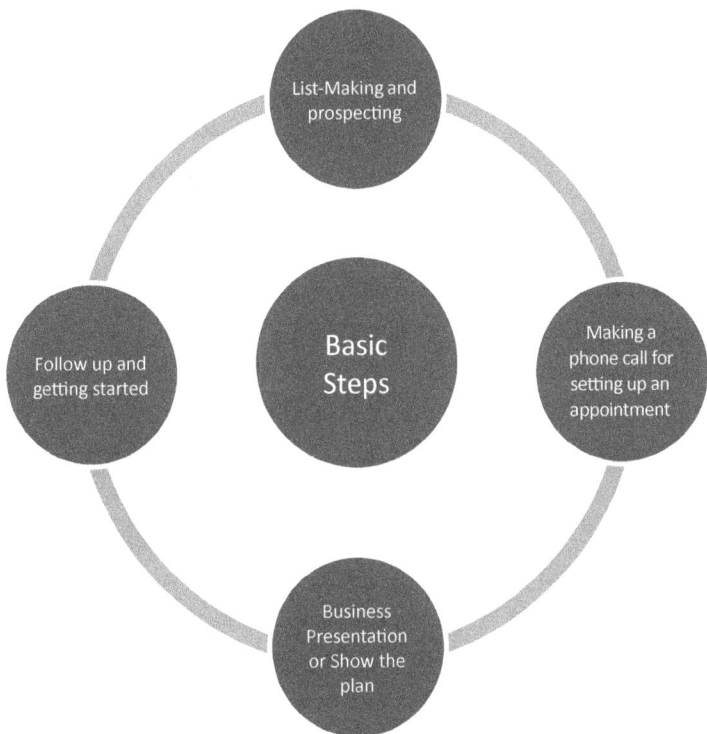

1. List-Making and Prospecting

This is the most important basic step. Do it wholeheartedly. It is the first step that a new person takes when he enters the business. In order to build your business, you need to get people see your business presentation. For this, you need to write down a list of names of people whom you know.

List is the raw material for building your business. You know how important is the supply of raw material required to run a production process smoothly. Without the raw material, no factory can run. Here, in Network Marketing Business, everything depends on how much raw material you have in the form of a list of names. Make a list of all the people whom you know without pre-judging anyone.

Remember, if you don't show your business to somebody, someone else will. Don't take decisions for others whether they'll get into the business or not. Take down all the names. Scan through your mobile phone contacts, your contacts on social networking platforms who are in touch with you, look at all the business cards you've collected, go through the wedding album, Facebook, Instagram, Twitter friends and followers and other sources of pictures.

Make a list of at least 200-250 names along with their contact details, work details, age and income. Build three lists. Local, Long Distance and International list separately. Keep on adding names and other details to your list as you get more names. It's a continuous process. Keep on adding names in the bottom and delete names from the top whom you have established contact with or shown the business presentation.

Mention a small note of the status of that call in the remarks section of the list-making pad. The list-making pad has the following columns:

a. Name
b. Phone number
c. Address
d. Age group
e. Profession and approx. income
f. Relation with you
g. Remarks

There are numerous other ways of name collection. You can write a blog and collect data about all the people who like your blog. Use memory joggers to help you recall names. Meanwhile, continue to cultivate a relationship with new people whom you meet daily for example during the morning walk, at the store, petrol pump, ATM, etc. List-making is the basic raw material of building a Network.

Don't commit the typical mistake of not writing names and telling your sponsor that it's in your head or writing a few names. Write down enough names on the list pad. When adequate raw material is there, there will not be any delay in further processes. Prospecting is a technique wherein you can talk to anyone and add their name in the list.

Prospecting helps in searching for potential customers with the intention of developing new business with them. When you master the skills of prospecting, you can add any number of names to your list. You can talk to even strangers and check their interest. Having big numbers in the list adds to your self-image. You will not worry even if some people say 'No'. You know you can add more names.

2. Making a Phone call for setting up an appointment

This sounds the most difficult thing to do for a new person or even those who are there for quite some time. Making a phone call sounds a hurricane task. But this is a very important step. By making a phone call you establish contact with your prospect to set up an appointment for showing the business presentation.

You can take the help of your sponsor and uplines to make the initial phone calls on your behalf. Listen to them carefully while they make the call. Understand how they begin, the script and answer objections. When you have understood the entire process of a phone call, you may even write down the script on a piece of paper and practice it before making your calls. Your script should be short.

Remember, the purpose of making the phone call is to set an appointment and not for discussing business over the phone. Do not attempt to answer too many questions on the phone call. Your call should not exceed 1 minute. Tell the other person that you would answer all the questions during the course of the business presentation. Just check their interest and invite them for the presentation. You can use different scripts depending upon the profession of the prospect. The more phone calls you make, the more perfection you'll get. While making phone calls, usually you follow two approaches:

- **Curious Approach**
  This approach is a more convenient approach when you are new in the business. In this approach, while making the phone call, you create curiosity in the mind of the prospect by asking indirect questions and checking their interest. You do not tell anything about the business. This approach brings good results. This approach is quite useful if you are using social media as a tool for contacting.

- **Direct Approach**
  In this approach, you directly expose the business to the prospect. This approach is useful when you have spent some time in the business and understand the business. The direct approach is useful where people whom you want to contact know that you are already doing this business successfully. Here, you can handle the objections raised by the prospects by giving tactical replies.

  Initially, while making the phone calls, you may feel some fear and hesitation. You will feel butterflies in your stomach. It is pretty normal. It has happened to me. It happens to every networker. You're not alone. Figure out a way to overcome that.

Focus on your dreams and goals. Why have you come to this business? What are your goals? What kind of lifestyle do you perceive for yourself after a few years of grinding work? Your dreams will give you power. When the dream is big enough, facts don't count.

Develop Giving Attitude

While making the phone call always remember that you are going to give something to the other person and not taking anything from them. If they come to the business, their life is going to change, they will fulfil their dreams and goals.

You're helping them achieve something in life through this business. Always believe in giving to others, serving others. When they will be successful in this business, they would be very grateful for receiving the phone call that changed everything for them and their family.

Secondly, you are not promising them anything. You are just inviting them to see the business presentation. Tell them upfront that you are not going to sell anything to them. So, you need to be very excited to make the phone calls. Always keep your posture high while making phone calls.

Setting a target

Set a target for yourself in terms of how many calls per day you will make. Numbers have magic. They never lie and fail. When you give yourself a target, your mind starts working towards it. Always remember the law of average works everywhere with numbers. When you are constantly adding names to your list, you need not worry about who says what.

Phone Call Meeting

I've used this technique often and got wonderful results. Once a week, we gather new business owners at one place and ask them to bring their goal sheet for the phone calls. I call it the Phone Call Meeting.

The leader motivates the team and shares his experience of the phone call meetings held previously. He gives them a reward by announcing the time for the business presentation where he would show the plan. Then, he makes all the new people sit in different places in the room and ask them to make phone calls and note down the numbers and response. Set the appointment for the date and time that the leader has announced. This encourages the team to make phone calls.

There is a competitive environment in the room as everyone wants to excel. I have seen that phone call meetings have always produced great results. It enhances team spirit and develops a good relationship amongst new business owners. The excitement in the room is electrifying and encouraging. In the end, the leader declares the winner and rewards them with some books or other tools.

When we take feedback of the new people who attended the meeting for the first time and made the phone calls, they all say that their self-belief has gone up. I've observed that many people who could not otherwise make phone calls, start making the phone calls in the Phone Call Meeting and begin to set appointments.

3. Business Presentation or Show the Plan

This is the most exciting step of building the business and an important one too. The purpose of showing the business presentation is to give the facts and figures of your business to the prospects and help them make a decision. If you are new to the business, the plan will be shown by your sponsor or upline and you need to learn by watching them doing that.

The faster you learn to show the plan, the better it is. You are the owner of your own business. Only when you start showing the plan yourself, it is your business. Until then, it is the upline's business because you are dependent on them.

After all, you can love riding a horse only when you command the reins in your hands. Learn fast to show your own plan. It does not matter how bad your first plan is, just show your first plan. Your 20th plan will be better than your first plan but for that, you need to show nineteen plans. Your 20th plan cannot be your first plan.

> ➢ It does not matter who is showing the plan, what matters the most is who is seeing the plan.

It does not matter how great your plan is, what matters is how many plans you showed. The one who shows maximum plans grows much faster in this business. There are various ways of showing the plan. People now show the plan on Skype, Zoom and video calls.

1. **One on One**

   When you show the plan to someone sitting in front of you and there is no one else there, it is called one on one plan. Normally, it is done for working-class people coming straight from the office or for people whom we are meeting for the first time.

2. **Showing the plan to a couple**

   When you show the plan to a couple either at your house or their house or at a fixed place. Make sure that you also go there as a couple. If you are single, take the help of your uplines.

3. **Conducting a home meeting**

   When the meeting is conducted in a home, it is called a home meeting. The guests here are usually friends, family and neighbours. When you conduct a home meeting and your guests are more than 3-4 people, it is advisable to use a whiteboard or a flip chart and marker.

4. **Open meeting**

   Open Meeting is conducted in an auditorium or a big hall. Here, the plan is usually shown by successful leaders. Such meetings are conducted once in a week, preferably on weekends, so that anyone can invite guests there.

5. **Quick Overview**

   A quick overview is done to give a quick insight into the business when the time is short. Usually, it is done in 10 minutes. If the person shows interest, you may invite them to another meeting.

6. **Conducting a live session**

   You may take advantage of technology and conduct live sessions for business presentations. There are numerous tools available online now which can be effectively used to make the presentation. It is very conducive for building overseas business or building the business long distance. Later, once they join the business, you may connect them to local open meeting sessions near them.

While showing the plan, you need to take care of some important points. Some of these are:

1. Show the plan and not tell the plan.
2. The plan should be shown only after setting a proper appointment.
3. You need to be there on time for showing the plan.
4. If you have promised to show the plan for your team, reach there before time to ease out their tension.
5. Do not show long plans. Your plan should not exceed 45 minutes.
6. Always dress up for the occasion. You are the owner of your own business.
7. Always conduct the plan professionally.
8. The plan should be simple but engaging.
9. Your body language while showing the plan should be assertive.
10. Avoid any kind of distractions during your presentation.
11. Don't show the plan to the same person again and again. There is no point in chasing.

4. Follow up and getting started

Follow up starts immediately after showing the plan. The purpose of follow up is to help your person take the decision. There is a wonderful technique called "Jump through the window". When the prospect has seen the presentation, his mind is open. You need to enter his mind before it is closed. Try to reach on the other side of the window and help him make the decision.

Follow up is done to clear any question or doubt of the prospect. It is an important step. Those who want to join the business immediately, help them get started. Those who want to take some time, give them some business literature and set the next meeting time.

Follow up doesn't mean chasing people. Maintain your posture. Let the prospect take his own decision. Your job is only to guide them for taking the decision by providing them with the information they seek. Ask positive follow up questions.

Most of the times I've noticed that people in the business try to convince the prospect to join the business. My take is different and opposite on this. Rather than we convincing the prospects, they need to convince us as to why we would invest our time, money and energy on them.

What are the dreams that they want to achieve? There isn't any point in convincing prospects. We need to assist them in building the business if they take the decision to get in. Never ever get defensive with your prospect.

I've experienced that either people don't do follow up or they don't do it the right way. It's a very crucial step of decision making on the part of the prospect and you need to assist them in taking a decision of joining the business.

We, as leaders know how badly that person needs this business but the point is do they realize that? We need to make them realize the need. There are some fundamental things that you need to take care while doing follow up with the prospect.

1. Never disagree with your prospect over any point. You need to agree to disagree. Whenever a prospect raises any objection, do not immediately negate it. That will hurt their ego. Instead, first, agree that they are right. That satisfies their ego and they calm down. Then you can say what you know about that point.

2. Use people skills while dealing with your prospect. You need to be calm and composed. No need to get excited or agitated.
3. Use the magical technique of feel, felt and found. It works effectively.
4. Ask questions based on the format "why, what, how and what if/now what".
5. You need to be a good listener. Listen to your prospect with keenness. Show genuine interest in the person while listening.
6. Always remember that **people may not get in the business knowing what you do, but they join your business knowing why you do what you do.**
7. Never close the door on anybody.

You need to master yourself on the four basic steps that we discussed above. The more efficient and quicker you become in completing the cycle of the four basics, the bigger will be your business. In Network Marketing Business, your success is guaranteed if you follow the basic steps religiously. These steps are the sure-shot way to success.

Just to recapitulate....

➲ By performing the basic steps, you lay the foundation of a strong, long-term and profitable business. When the foundation is strong, the business will be sustainable and rewarding.

➲ The four basic steps help in faster growth in the Network Marketing Business. The faster you complete the cycle, the more profitable will be your business.

➲ Make prospecting your daily habit. List of names is the raw material for expanding the business. Prospecting helps in increasing the list.

➲ Learn to make phone calls. Phone call meetings can help new people in shedding fear. Take feedback.

➲ The one who shows more plans will have a bigger business. Showing the plan is the most exciting step of four basics.

➲ Help new people take the decision to build the business. Give them relevant literature for reference.

Scribble your Notes

CHAPTER 8

Becoming Core

Discipline is being able to force
yourself to do something, in spite
of how you feel, over and over until
it becomes a habit.

-KIM BRENNEMAN

By now you must've understood the potential of this business and what it can offer you if you build it the right way. We've already discussed what needs to be done to be successful in Network Marketing Business.

In the previous chapter, we discussed the basic steps to be followed in building this business. If your 'why' is clear and your goals are right in front of your eyes and you've been speaking your goals to yourself, it means you're on your way. Most of the people who do not succeed in the Network Marketing Business never reach up to this point. They may spend any amount of time, maybe years, but still, they don't make it. Some of the reasons we have discussed in the previous chapters.

> Winners don't make excuses and those who make, they never win.

I've seen many people not taking this business seriously. They will have one reason or the other to procrastinate.

Some of them would say, "I will do this business but let me get some free time since I am already busy in other activities."

Let me be straightforward in telling that free time would never come.

You need to build this business by taking out some time from your busy schedule. If you have goals unfulfilled and you want to achieve them, then you need to devote time to build this business by taking out some time. This business is for busy people because they understand the importance of time and its management more than anyone else.

Busy and successful people understand (ROTI), Return on Time Invested better than many others.

This is not for free people who have plenty of free time doing nothing. Those who do nothing will not do anything here as well. We are looking for hungry people who are hungry to achieve something worthwhile in their lives and are ready to grind it out.

When people tell that they don't have time to build this business, my reply to them is very simple. That is why you need this business more than I need.

Do you want to get the freedom of time to do the things you wish to do and you are not able to do currently because you are busy? You need to be honest and truthful to yourself. Let me share a story in this context and then we'll move forward:

Up in the Sky...

There was a football club which was working extremely hard to win the championship of that year. There were three months to go for the tournament to start. The club had many aspiring footballers who wanted to play in the final eleven. After many practice sessions, the coach selected 16 probables to start intensive training. Five more were selected for the bench strength.

The story begins from a footballer who was amongst those five selected only for bench strength. This young boy named Ronak desperately wanted to be in the playing eleven, but he was not even in the 16 selected for intensive training. The coach had already selected the best footballers. Ronak would often go up to his coach and ask him what improvement he needs.

The coach always told him, "You are a bit slow in running as compared to those who have been selected."

All the 21 players started practising but special attention was paid to the selected 16.

Finally, the tournament started and league matches began. The club started rising on the points table and at the end of the league matches, this club topped in their pool and they were to play for the first semi-final with the top team of the other pool. The team was working very hard for the semi-final match. A day before the semi-final match, Ronak got the news that his father was sick and hospitalized. His condition was serious. He had to leave the club with a heavy heart to see his father. The team bid him farewell and he wished the team good luck for the semi-final.

When Ronak reached hospital to see his ailing father, doctors briefed him that he had a cardiac arrest and his condition was deteriorating further. Doctors tried their best but could not save his father.

Ronak was deeply broken. With a heavy heart, he did all the rituals and cremated his father. All this while, his mind and heart were with his team that had advanced into the finals of the championship by beating the opponent team in a closely fought semi-final.

The final was fixed for a week later. After going through all the rituals, Ronak returned back to his club to be with them during the final match, which was now only three days far.

All his teammates were in shock to hear about his father's demise. They remembered how his father was always present with the team as a spectator in the audience and encouraged and motivated the team during the league matches before falling sick.

Finally, the day arrived for the final between the two best teams. The match started and there was huge excitement amongst the spectators cheering for their respective teams.

Ronak sat in the dugout cheering for his team. That day, the opponent team was playing great football and they scored 2 goals in the first half. The scoreboard stated 0-2. Ronak's team was trailing by two goals.

The coach made several changes in the first half but all went in vain. During the half time, in the team briefing, the mood was sombre but the coach and other staff tried to lift the morale of the players.

Ronak went to his coach and asked if he could play for some time in the second half. His coach gracefully declined him fully understanding his state of mind having lost his father only last week. He pleaded but the coach did not agree.

The second half started and within the first 10 minutes, the opponent team scored another goal. The score now stood at 0-3.

The coach was running around in a pensive mood trying to encourage and direct his team playing inside. He made another change. For the next five minutes, there was a fierce battle to score a goal from both teams. The big clock showed only 30 minutes left in the match for the final whistle to blow.

The coach was losing hope by the passing of every minute. He didn't know what to do next. Just then one of his strikers got injured on the ground and needed medical treatment. Ronak came up to his coach again and pleaded to send him in. The coach saw tears of determination in his eyes. All his plans had already been exhausted and there was no hope of revival.

He thought, "What this boy would do even if he is sent in?" He had not played league matches and practised with the team as standby only.

Finally, seeing no other option, he decided to send Ronak in, replacing his injured player playing in the forward position. Ronak touched the ground and went in.

That evening Ronak ran with electrifying speed.

Within the next two minutes, he got a pass from his teammate and he ran with the football moving forward in the opponent's half. Controlling the ball and running fast, he reached in-front of the opponent's goal post. He looked around for his striker but he was not there.

In the split of that second, he kicked the ball with all his might from that position because other team's defenders were around him trying to snatch the ball. The ball sailed into the nets defeating the fetching hands of the opponent goalkeeper. He had scored the first goal for his team.

There was an uproar in the spectators and his all teammates congratulated him. The score was 1-3; with the time clock showing 24 minutes to go for the whistle.

Now, fast movements could be seen on the ground and both teams demonstrated magical footballing skills. Ronak was extremely charged up and shouted a lot, motivating his team to play the best football.

Minutes later, another opportunity was created and Ronak passed the ball to the striker beating the opponent players. The striker kicked the ball in the goalpost. Ronak was instrumental in that goal as his pass came right at the crucial time and place. Now, the score stood at 2-3.

The opposition team started playing delaying tactics with long passes and corners. They were not willing to give the ball to the other team. Time was running out. Ronak wanted to take possession of the ball and create an opportunity, but he was denied the ball by the opposition. 4-5 minutes passed and nothing spectacular happened on the field.

Suddenly, a misfired header from one of the centre forward of the other team was intercepted well by Ronak.

He moved like a racing machine from his position, negotiating the opposing defenders and entered the other half from the side. He gave a pass and got a reverse pass from his partner. He negotiated the ball well for a few more seconds. Spectators were up, on their feet, seeing another opportunity to a goal being created.

Ronak positioned himself well in the opponent's D, he kicked the ball which went straight into the nets of the goal.

Wow! He had scored yet another goal for his team.

There was a buzz in the air. The coach was bewildered to see the kind of football that Ronak was playing that night.

Probably, he was playing the football of his life. The Coach had never seen him playing that kind of football, ever before. He never rated him higher than the others, but that day Ronak had brought excitement back into the team. A couple of good moves by the opposing team were negated by Ronak's team. Time was ticking away.

Both teams were looking for the winning goal as the score stood level at 3-3. The crowd screamed for their respective teams.

Eleven players from each team were trying their best to strike one winning goal. But that night, Ronak stood above all.

He had completely transformed the game in the second half for his team. The team, which once, had almost lost hope of winning, was just one goal away from winning the championship. Months of rigorous training and practice were culminating into a Grand Finale.

Ronak wanted to be the hero that night and displayed brilliant footballing skills in the short period for which he was in. Nonetheless, he had not finished as yet. He was playing with a mission.

Two to three opposition players were always around Ronak and not letting him go forward. Last five minutes were left in the match. Both teams tried desperately. The climax was being created. The final few minutes for the whistle to blow and then both the teams will play for 15 minutes of extra play to bring out the result.

In the final few minutes, Ronak created an opportunity but the opposing team, understanding the danger, blocked him by pushing him on his chest and side-lined the ball. Referee fully understood the motive of the assault on Ronak and awarded a corner to Ronak's team. It was opposed but the referee didn't yield.

Minutes before the final whistle, the coach decided for Ronak to take the corner instead of the striker. The coach had by then well understood that it was Ronak's day.

Ronak positioned himself at the corner, saw the field and players from both teams positioned there. He saw all his strikers and headers near the goalpost. He looked towards the sky, prayed and then kicked the football with great power. The football took a nice flight and curve, passed all the players defending and as they watched, the ball sailed into the goalpost.

It was a Goal!

A decider in the final minutes! Wow! That was just an unbelievable strike!! Straight into the Goalpost!!!

Ronak, an underrated player had brought victory to his team. Everyone was astonished. His team lifted him up. He was the hero of the match that night. Within a few seconds, the referee blew the final whistle.

The score stood 4-3 in favour of Ronak's Team. What a moment that was!

The team celebrated the victory. Spectators were thrilled and excited as they had witnessed a wonderful game of football. The coaches were happy. Everyone was talking about only one man, Ronak. What a great game of football he had played and displayed that night!

It was a long night of dance and celebration for the club that day. Celebrations went deep into the night. All his teammates were singing praises for Ronak. It was but for him that the club had won the championship. The coach also praised Ronak for the unbelievable footballing skills that he had displayed. Everyone wondered how he overcame his emotions as he had just lost his father a few days before.

Then, with tears in his eyes, Ronak broke the story. He told everyone that his father was very passionate about his son playing football for the club and winning the championship. That is why he always came to see his team playing. He always cheered from the audience to buck up his son and the team to do well.

Ronak told everyone that he had always lied to his father that he was playing in the game whereas he was not. In all league matches, he sat outside in the dugout while his father, sitting amongst the spectators, thought that he was playing with the team.

Ronak told them that he lied to his father all the time because he could not see. He was a blind man. There was a pin drop silence there. Emotions started to roll down.

With tears in his eyes, he told them that when his father died, he knew that he was all the time lying to his father. When he came back to the team, he pleaded with the coach many times to let him play. The coach did not allow. He was crying sitting in the dugout. But when he got the chance, he wanted to be honest to himself and his father, for now, he could see from up in the sky, see his son playing football. He did not lie to his father that night.

* * *

Friends, the purpose of sharing this story is to make you realize that you need to be honest to yourself. Network Marketing Business has come to you as blessings from God. You're very fortunate that somebody has shown you the business and you've said yes to it. You need to make it big and make it count.

This is a very simple and pure business. The business is built on complete honesty and integrity. There are leaders who are willing to help you realize your dreams. They are ready to invest in you. You need to be ready for it.

Network Marketing Companies started in India around 1995. Many companies have grown successfully in this business and many new companies are growing. These companies work in different product categories and there are a large number of distributors of these companies who are building the business. This business has a huge potential to grow and a company's growth is bound by the growth of its business owners.

> **You are very fortunate that somebody has shown you the business and you have said yes to it. You need to make it big and make it count. This is a very simple and pure business. The business is built on complete honesty and integrity. There are leaders who are willing to help you realize your dreams. They are ready to invest in you. You need to be ready for it.**

The companies are investing heavily on plants, infrastructure, brand positioning, and distributor friendly atmosphere. The biggest benefit to the business owners is that they need not invest to create infrastructure for themselves in terms of office, delivery of products, research or anything else. It is taken care of by their parent company.

Network Marketing gives the opportunity to an ordinary person to become a businessman. Isn't it a wonderful opportunity? So, effectively there are four pillars on which a successful business can be built. They are –

1. Manufacturing Company
2. The system supporting the business owners
3. Your line of sponsorship
4. And 'You'

All other pillars are strong and ready to help you in building the business. The only pillar in the question is the 4th one that is 'you'. Are you ready? If you are not, your upline can easily replace you with someone else. So, who needs to be ready? It is you.

Steps to becocming the core

When you decide to build this business, the first thing is to become core. The core is the central or primary driving force of the business. So, this is the person who does all the basics to the best of his/her efforts and is in the good books of his upline. Uplines can count on him. He is accountable for his work and words.

Leaders in this business always like core distributors or business owners and want to work with them. The core people move fast in this business and grow big time. All the leaders who have big businesses in Network Marketing Business have first become core distributors. In the Network Marketing business, core means a combination of Association, Character Building and Work Ethic.

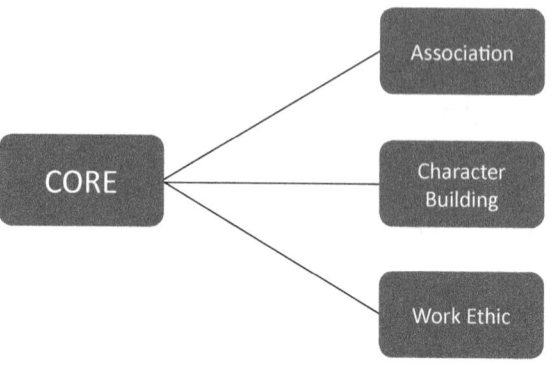

Association

The first thing is to increase your association. Here, association means association with the successful leaders, books and audio/video talks. You should attend each and every meeting/seminar/webinar/live session that you are eligible for. Make no excuses.

> ➤ People who don't go, they don't grow. People who are in, they win.

Read books which your upline and the system promote to you. You get wisdom from books. You can have successful people right there with you in your car, at your home or anywhere you go. Listen to their audio/video talks. In those talks, they share their knowledge and experience. The speakers in these talks are successful networkers who have big teams but they all started from the scratch. By listening to them, you get to know how they built such a big business. You can apply these learnings in building your organization.

Character Building

This is a very important step in becoming core. Your upline wants you to keep your word, always be teachable and accountable and always in communication with them. This makes you predictable and trustworthy. You should always be ready to learn and listen. First build yourself and then teach others. You cannot teach others if you yourself don't follow that. Always remember, this is the business of duplication. You duplicate what you do.

Work Ethic

This is the action part of becoming core. It is the working zone. Always be the first customer of your own business. That makes business sense. You should be 100% user of all the products that your company deals in and that you want to flow in your network to come. Remember, people will do what you do and not what you say.

When you use the products, you can recommend it to others and make them your customers. Share your knowledge about your product usage with your potential clients to convert them into your customers. Give them service. The bigger the customer base, the greater the volume you will do. Once you become 100% user and retailer, the next step is to start building your network. Your network is the result of the business plans that you show. But remember, your network will do what you do and teach them to do. There has to be sync in that. If you don't yourself do what you teach, people will not follow you.

To enumerate the core principles, each section consists of three components. Let me list it down for your comfort.

Becoming Core - Build yourself on Association, Character Building and Work Ethic

Association

1. Book Reading
2. Listening to Audio and Video of successful people
3. Attending business seminars and meetings

Character Building

4. Being always ready for learning, be teachable
5. Always in communication with growing upline
6. Be Accountable for who you are

Work Ethic

7. Become a customer of your own business
8. Service some customers for retail sales
9. Showing Business Presentation

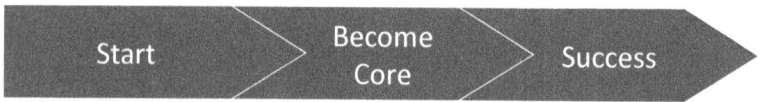

In Network Marketing, money comes from individual volume and the volume generated by your network. Let us understand that.

There are three steps by which you make money in Network Marketing

1. Self-Consumption of products
2. Retailing the products to your customers
3. Network volume

Now, if you don't perform the first two steps correctly, how will you duplicate it in your network? I told you, your network will do what you do. They are watching you. If they watch you doing the first two steps, automatically they will follow and do it. But if they don't see you doing the first two steps, duplication becomes difficult. That is why this step in becoming core is called work ethic and not simply work. Ethic means doing the right way. Is your work ethic duplicable? Only that will determine how big your network is going to be.

When you start this business, your aim is to focus on becoming core. Do whatever it takes to become core because the real journey towards your goals begins here. Check with your sponsor and upline team and find out what are the steps you need to follow and the action plan needed to become core. You enjoy special training sessions and motivation from your leaders when you become core.

Dress up for Success

Dressing up for success is very critical and carries a lot of weightage. As they say, the first impression is the last impression. You should be dressed up for the occasion. In the Network Marketing business, the only investment that you need to make is on yourself. Rest of the investments are taken care of by the parent company.

You are the one who is actually presenting and demonstrating the business to the people. Dressing up does not only mean the kind of clothes you wear but also the kind of attitude you carry. A smile on the face is also part of dressing up. Facial expressions attract people towards you.

A recent study suggests that first impressions are done in the first seven seconds of meeting someone. And you thought does dressing up make sense when there is so much buzz in the air about smart casuals? Actually, it does matter in this business. Moreover, it helps in raising your own image. In my training programs, when I am explaining about self-image, dress up and attitude, I always ask a few questions from my audience.

How do you feel on the day of your birthday? How do you dress yourself up that particular day? How is your mindset? What attitude do you carry that day? How do you respond when people greet you on that day? Is there any dull moment that day?

Almost everyone says that they feel great on the day of their birthday. Why is it so? Why can't we carry the same attitude every single day?

The purpose of asking these questions is to make them understand the concept of dressing up. Always dress up for the occasion. If you are in the business meeting, your attire should be a business dress. If you are at a party, your dress can be a party dress. But you can't go to a business meeting wearing a party dress. Albeit, you may wear a nice length suit and still go to a party.

Recently, in one of my conferences, I was impressing upon the point of dressing nicely. I asked everyone a question, "How many of you like chocolate?" All of them raised their hands and said, "Yes, we do like chocolate."

I called up one volunteer on the stage sitting in the first few rows and asked him, "What do you like the most in chocolate?" He was a little confused in answering the question.

I asked the audience. Somebody said the taste, others said the love in the chocolate, and another said it all depends on who is giving you the chocolate and so on. One young couple sitting in the audience said what they liked the most is to unwrap the chocolate. I told them all these are important but the most important thing in the chocolate is its packing or wrapper. The chocolates are always packed most elegantly and in an attractive manner.

Now I asked the audience, "Would you like to eat the same chocolate that you love the most if it is wrapped in a dirty, crumpled piece of old newspaper?" Everyone shouted "No".

I said here is the point. It doesn't matter howsoever great and profitable the business may be, what matters the most is who is representing it. It all depends on you how you carry this business to the people. They first see you and not the business.

In the Network Marketing business, you need to be ready to contact and prospect your next big networker of the future. For that, you need to look nice. Before moving out of your home, stand in front of a life-size mirror and ask yourself, "Do I look like a businessman?" It's equally true for women in the business as well.

Take some special time out for yourself to remind you and prepare you for the next business activity. You are the showroom of your business. Your dress, attitude, walk, facial expressions and your confidence and style must impress everyone you meet.

Just to recapitulate....

➲ There is no scope of procrastination in this business. The best time to build the business is NOW; you will never get free time to build it. You need to identify the reasons to build this business.

➲ You need to be honest to yourself. Make a commitment to building this business for meeting the needs and desires of your family.

➲ Of the four pillars, three are strong and ready to support you. The fourth pillar is you. You need to be ready. Check with your leaders on how to become 'core' in the business.

➲ You need to dress up for success. How you carry yourself is very important in this business.

➲ You need to be ready to meet your next prospect who is going to make a big business.

Scribble your Notes

CHAPTER 9

Powers at Your Disposal

Words spoken have the power to
change, modify or manipulate... A
wise will think and speak... But a
fool will speak and repent.

-SHEBA KATAPUR

No other business concept on the face of this earth can teach you things that you learn while building Network Marketing Business. This concept has impacted so many lives across the globe in a better way.

This should, in fact, be a subject matter of research. The kind of hand-holding that you get in this business is unparalleled. I always tell people that the basic difference between a traditional business and network marketing business is that while in traditional businesses you first see it and then do whereas in this business you first do and then see. The principles that I learnt, the powers which I practised and mastered in this business have truly impacted my life.

➢ Look at the finished products of this business, the successful leaders, and you'll see what they've become from what they were when they started.

There is a complete transformation of the many persons through this business. With God's grace, I'm one of the lucky ones who became a better person in the last twenty years all because of this business.

The end result of any business must not be ascertained by what a man gets from it rather from the fact that what he became through it. I owe it to my mentors. I am privileged that I've personally been mentored by some of the finest and greatest people of this industry. I am what I'm today all because of the great hand-holding I got from such great servers of the Network Marketing Business.

Many times, I wonder, how can some people say 'No' to this business? It is such a beautiful and rewarding business.

They won't ever know what they said 'No' to. I feel Goosebumps when I think what if I had said 'No' to this business. In traditional businesses, just make one mistake and you may incur irreparable losses. But in this business, every day is a new day and a new hope. You may have done something drastically wrong yesterday, but you can start afresh today provided you have learnt from that mistake. It is such a forgiving business.

> ➢ I pray to God that you live enough in this business and personally feel what great leaders of this business have felt, become what they have become, achieve what they have achieved and enjoy the life that they are enjoying.

Powers for you

When you invest your time in the Network Marketing Business, it multiplies and gives you manifold returns. You learn the principles of success and you become a better person. People around you start noticing that change in you. Whatever you do outside this business, you excel there as well because those principles are not confined to this business only. They work everywhere.

Let me share with you some of the powers that will help you to build a huge business. These powers will help you overcome any obstacle that may come your way while building this business. You need to let these powers sink in you and become a part of you so that you can reap rich dividends.

1. Power of Association

The whole is always greater than the sum total of all its parts. This is a very powerful statement and needs to be understood. In general terms, we can rephrase this. A single finger of the hand is less powerful than all the fingers clubbed together to form a fist. To simplify it further, take an apple, cut it into 4 pieces. Now join all the four pieces. Does it make a complete apple? No. Theoretically, the apple is complete but not as the original one.

This signifies that whole is always greater than the sum total of all its parts. There's power in the wholeness. That's what power of Association does for you in Network Marketing Business which, otherwise, you can't ever do alone. Big decisions are made in big functions when people rise up to the occasion and relate with the surroundings.

Big functions are the result of the power of association. Even the critics of the business get mesmerized when they attend big rallies and see the excitement there. That is why functions and seminars are instrumental in the growth of leaders and the business. When a new person enters that arena, he feels that pulsating excitement and jubilation which he may not have experienced before.

Together, a team can achieve more success because every team member contributes to each other's success. This is a participative success. The growth of your business can be measured by the growing numbers of your team from function to function. Teams that stay together always grow big time. So, always stay united with your leader and system.

2. Power of Submission

True mentorship is possible only when you are in absolute submission with your mentor. Submission means absence of rebellion. When you submit to your upline, their responsibility towards you increases. Submission is not a sign of weakness rather it's a sign of strength.

Many times, the meaning of the word submission is construed upon wrongly. It is not lowering yourself in front of someone. It is actually deriving powers of the other person. In your line of sponsorship, find a successful leader with whom you relate and increase your association. Once both of you are comfortable, you can request for the mentorship guidance. This will help you to grow faster in the business with fewer mistakes. Mentorship is the strength of this business.

Always be in a submission mode with your growing upline in this business. Also, remember that this is the business of the duplication. Your team is watching you doing things. People follow those who follow someone. To be an effective leader, always be in submission with your uplines.

3. Power of Spoken Words

Words are like seeds. They grow up to be big plants. So, choose your words wisely. Think twice before you speak. Our words can change our destiny, so better keep a watch on them. We need to be mindful of what we speak.

There is power in the words that we speak. So always speak what you want and not what you don't want or what you have. You can create a life of your choices by using the proven principle of the power of spoken words. You just need to learn what to speak. Speak your future in the present. When you speak, you're the closest one who is listening and that too with both your ears. Everything that you speak is first going into your brain and you know brain processes information. So, you are your first listener.

I always guide people that if you want to change the way you live, you need to do two things

➤ Change the way you think
➤ Change the way you speak

If you learn to make these two changes, you can achieve anything you desire; be it health, wealth, happiness, relationships or success.

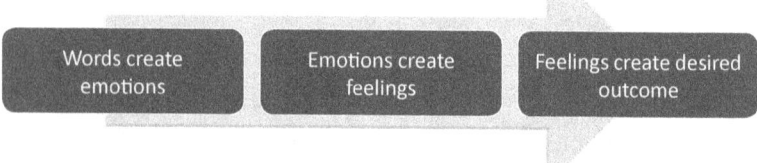

Words create emotions → Emotions create feelings → Feelings create desired outcome

As explained in chapter five when we discussed Self-Talk, speak your goals and that will strengthen your feelings to bring the desired outcome into existence. Create positive affirmations for yourself and your goals and use the power of spoken words to generate the right emotions in you to start working towards achieving your goals. Always make conscious efforts to speak the words that build you up and take you a step closer to your dreams.

In my workshops on NLP (Neuro-Linguistic Programming) and Power of Subconscious Mind, I always lay stress on the way a person thinks and what he speaks. If a person is able to master and control these two things, they can turnaround their life completely.

I know this is an entirely different topic which is outside the purview of this book, but still, I would like to discuss a few things from the network marketing business perspective.

The basic reason for coming into the network marketing business is to fulfil dreams and desires. The universe has abundant powers and it can fulfil all your dreams and desires. The only thing is we should know how to seek the powers of the universe to help us achieve our dreams. Life always has its own way of teaching us by making sure we suffer immensely from not following the laws of the universe. Let me explain this by way of a story:

A little boy living in the hills with his mother had a fight with her. In anger, he ran out of the house and stood on the edge of a valley overlooking a big mountain. In anger, he shouted, "I hate you." His voice echoed in the valley and it came back as "I hate you", "hate you" ...

The boy had not experienced this before and he got scared. He came back home terrified and lay in his mother's lap. His mother could fathom that something was wrong with the child. She asked him and he narrated the whole story. He said that there lived a monster in the valley who spoke back to him in anger.

His mother knew what had transpired with him. She took him out holding his hand to the same spot. The child was petrified. She consoled him and told him to shout loudly "I love you". He shouted and the voice echoed back saying "I love you" "Love you" ....

The child was in a dilemma. Both of them came back home and the mother taught the child a lesson of the powers of the universe.

She told him that whatever you give to the universe, it gives you back the same thing in abundance. If you spread anger, it is going to come back to you stronger and if you spread love, it is also going to come back stronger. It's our choice what we seek from the universe.

It is called the Law of Mirrors. Mirror reflects exactly what you put in front of it. You look at the mirror with anger in your heart and you will see an angry face, on the contrary, if you look into the mirror with love in your heart, you will find a loving face.

The mirror never lies. It reflects only what you put forth. When we blame life for something wrong that has happened, it is as if blaming the mirror for reflecting our true self.

> **The universe has abundant powers and it can fulfil all your dreams and desires. The only thing is we should know how to seek the powers of the universe to help us achieve our dreams. Life always has its own way of teaching us by making sure we suffer immensely from not following the laws of the universe.**

If we want to achieve any specific goal or a target and we seek the power from the universe, the universe is going to give the power which will help us achieve our goal. First believe that it is possible then seek powers, after that receive powers and finally show gratitude by thanking the universe. These are precisely the steps.

This all can be done by formulating positive self-talk and using the power of spoken words and sending a signal to the universe. Trust me, this is magical and purely practical. Seek with a clean and pure heart and the universe is certainly going to bless you.

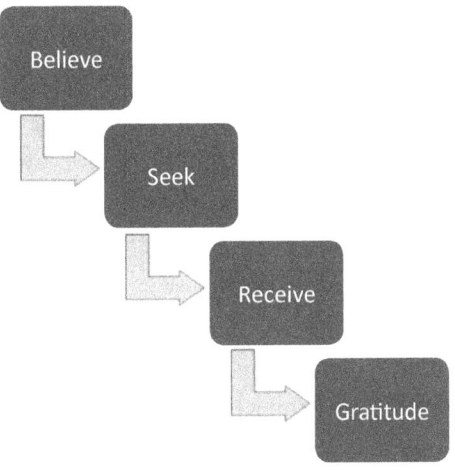

Showing gratitude is the biggest asset that you can acquire. Can you withdraw money from a bank if you have not deposited money into it? No. First, you make deposits and then withdrawal. Gratitude is the deposit with the God that you can withdraw when in need. Keep on adding more to it. There are millions of reasons for which we can thank God. This asset gives compounded returns. So always show gratitude.

Delayed Gratification

Delayed gratification means focusing on the process of sowing and allow the harvest to come at its right time. The tree will give fruits when it is meant to and not when we want them. Let me explain this important concept of Delayed Gratification through a famous Stanford University Experiment known as "The Marshmallow Experiment."

The Marshmallow Experiment

At the beginning of the 1960s, a Stanford University Professor Walter Mischel and his team of researchers conducted a series of important psychological studies by testing hundreds of children in the 4-5 years age group. The experiment began by bringing children into a room, making them sit on the chairs and placing a marshmallow on the table in front of each of them.

At this point in time, Walter offered a bargain or a deal to the children. He told them that he was going to leave the room for some time and if any of them didn't eat the marshmallow, then they would be rewarded with a second marshmallow. Only those who did not eat the marshmallow in his absence would be given the additional marshmallow. The deal was pretty simple: One treat right now or two treats later.

Walter left the children alone for 15 minutes and watched their footage later on. The footage of the children waiting in the room was quite entertaining. While some kids jumped up and ate their marshmallow as soon as Walter closed the door and went out, there were a few kids who waited, wiggled, bounced and scooted in their chairs as they tried to restrain themselves, but eventually gave in to the temptation a few minutes later.

And, finally, a few of the children did manage to wait and resist themselves for the entire time.

As the years passed, the children grew up. The team of researchers kept proper track of them and conducted follow up studies and measured each child's progress on a number of parameters. What they found was overwhelmingly surprising.

The children who were willing to delay gratification and waited to receive two marshmallows ended up having high scores in SAT, better grades, skills and better responses to stress as reported by their parents.

The team tracked and followed those kids for more than 40 years and found that the group that delayed their gratification succeeded in every sphere of life. In other words, this series of experiments and research established that the ability to delay gratification was critical for success in life.

Now, let us understand delayed gratification in the context of the Network Marketing Business. This business is not a quick-rich scheme that will make you a millionaire overnight. Most of the people who join this business come from those backgrounds where they had instant gratification, where you work and get paid for. Whether it is a job or traditional business, they work on the instant gratification. Nothing wrong with that.

Let us understand the difference. In the Marshmallow Experiment, the reward for a wait of just 15 minutes was just double. Though it was a bit difficult for the kids to resist the temptation, a few kids did that. Those who ate marshmallows and did not wait got only one. The biggest reward for delayed gratification is that you get more.

First of all, I am thankful to God that I got into a business where we were taught what delayed gratification is. It is not possible in a job. No wonder, no one will do a job if they are not paid for. In the US and many European Countries, many workers are paid weekly salaries. Daily wage earners are paid daily at the end of the day. There is nothing wrong in it and neither am I trying to put it down.

If a daily wage earner invests in his education in the evenings after the job and works extra hours to finance that, that investment of time and money is delayed gratification which is going to benefit him in the coming days. Investing time to get something bigger in future is delayed gratification.

Sowing and reaping principle also demonstrates the benefits of delayed gratification. For a handful of seeds that the farmer sows, he waits for the harvest time and gets more in the crop than what he had sown. In Network Marketing Business, if you are willing to invest your time and money and you are willing to learn and listen, you can have a decent cash flow in 2-3 years.

Law of Attraction

Law of attraction is one of the most powerful laws of the universe. The law states that whatever a human mind can conceive and believe, it can achieve. You're going to attract in your life whatever you focus on. This is a powerful law and it doesn't matter whether you know about it or not, the law still works.

Just like the law of gravity, if you don't know the law, the law will still be in force. If someone happens to fall from the building and get injured, he cannot claim that gravity shouldn't have worked on him since he did not know or study about it. The law will take its own course. Similarly, the law of attraction keeps on working irrespective of the fact that you know about it nor not. Like attracts like. You need to choose between everyday battles or blessings. Anything that you think expands. Choose wisely.

In Network Marketing Business, I teach people the power of visualisation which is based on the law of attraction. The universe will respond enthusiastically to the vibrations that you send through the power of visualisation. If your energy frequency is in alignment with what you want to attract in life, then the law of attraction will certainly help you in achieving the desired results. So, ask the universe what you want and not what you don't want. Always have a firm belief that you'll get what you want, work towards that direction and see the magic happening in your life.

I have attracted so many good things in my life by using this law effectively. Just to give you a sample of how I do it, let us take the example of this book in your hand that I've written. Now let us bring back here the why statement that I had written for myself to give you a sample example.

My 'why' statement is:

> *"To train, educate and empower people all over the world so that they can achieve what they desire and thereby improve their lives."*

Now, the purpose of writing this book is to share my experience of 20 years in Network Marketing Business so that it can train, educate and empower people all over the world so that they can achieve what they desire and thereby improve their lives.

Now, I believe you can connect the dots and understand the laws clearly. Here are some of the examples of the self-talk that I use and attract the powers of the universe through the power of visualisation. I can vividly see everything crystal clear right in front of my eyes.

Thank you, God, this book has served its purpose of empowering people to achieve their dreams.

Thank you, God, my book has attained the number one position in the best-selling book for network marketing in the world.

Thank you, God, you have made me a celebrity author and assigned me the duty to train, educate and empower people all over the world. I am blessed.

The quantum of hard work and discipline that God imbibed in me to finish this book in record time is just amazing. It was just beyond my reach. The powers of the universe helped me in putting massive action to complete the project well within time despite facing challenges. The powers helped me to stay on course and get the job done. Thank you, God, for everything.

Just to recapitulate....

➲ The kind of teachings and learning that we get in the Network Marketing Business is unparallel. People have been completely transformed in this business.

➲ When you invest your time and money in this business, it multiplies and gives you manifold returns.

➲ The principles and techniques that you learn in this business can be applied anywhere else as well. You become a better person in every aspect.

➲ Powers help you overcome your anxiety and challenges. Learn to make use of the powers and you will see miracles happening in your life.

➲ The Marshmallow Experiment by Prof. Walter Mischel and his team proved that the law of delayed gratification works.

➲ Whatever a human mind can conceive and believe, it can achieve. The Law of Attraction works irrespective of whether you know it or not. Powers of the universe help you in achieving your dreams and goals.

Scribble your Notes

PART V

Know your Products and handling objections

CHAPTER 10

Importance and Need for Products

Don't find customers for your products, find products for your customers.

-SETH GODIN

The concept of Selling

Selling is a concept which probably was born along with humans. Selling complements the need of the seller as well as the buyer. Selling is construed upon as a professional skill which can be attributed to only skilled sellers. This is a debatable topic.

Selling is so inherently rooted in us that we don't even know that we are actually selling. When a new Startup is presenting its idea to the venture capitalist, they're in fact selling their idea to convince the investor to invest in their Startup.

The company you work for must have a product or a service that it offers to its clients. You're working there and trading your skills for a payout. Is it not selling? Just ponder over it a bit. I was already a salesman selling my services in my job. Everybody is a salesman selling either some product or service.

With technological advancement, both products and services have undergone radical changes. Competition has become more intense. The customer has become more educated and informed and so are the choices. With the changing times, the sales force also needs to be more prepared and trained.

Myths broken

When I meet new people about the business, the common objection I find amongst them is that they don't want to sell products. They often say, "Selling is not my cup of tea." Honestly speaking, I was also like them prior to joining the Network Marketing Business.

When it comes to Network Marketing Business, why do you take selling so differently?

Network Marketing Business is a team business. While some distributors are good at sponsoring people, some are good at retailing the products to new customers. That is a balancing act. With more than 60% workforce in direct selling industry constitutin women entrepreneurs, selling becomes much easier as in Network Marketing recommendation and feedback works magically. Here, selling is one to one.

> **While some distributors are good at sponsoring people, some are good at retailing the products to new customers. That is a balancing act. With more than 60% work force in direct selling industry constituting women entrepreneurs, selling becomes much easier as in Network Marketing recommendation and feedback work magically. Here, selling is one to one. Satisfaction and feedback play a vital role.**

Satisfaction and feedback play a vital role. I often tell people that even though you don't like selling, can you guarantee that you'll not find a few people who love selling? That is what makes it interesting as a team business.

While discussing the topic 'selecting the right Network Marketing Company for yourself' in Chapter Two of this book, I explained that the company must have a unique product line to offer to the people. Products are the backbone of the Network Marketing Business. If a company is not having a product or a service and is luring you by offering big incentives, please double-check before joining. It can be an illegal money circulation scheme.

Understanding the products-The Business Sense

As a business owner, you must have complete knowledge about the products that the company is offering. The first thing that I did when I started this business was to understand the product range. Since I had started my own business, I first became a customer of my own business and started using the products. The thumb rule that I followed was pretty simple. Whenever my family needed some product, I would check if that was available through my business and ensured to buy from there only and not from the market. That makes business sense.

Be your own customer first. It will enhance your belief and give you the strength to share the products with others. Self-Use of the products is of utmost importance. You can't tell your team to use the products if you yourself don't not use them.

> People don't do what you say, they do what you do. This is the fundamental principle of duplication of this business.

Remember that the new guidelines of the Government prohibit Network Marketing Companies to charge money from people on recruitment. It's only through sales by you and your team that you'll make money, so remember your total volume is the sum total of your personal volume and the volume of the network. If your business has a thousand people but doing zero volume, your total volume will be zero and you'll not make any money, it's not about recruitment but about training and guidance. You'll teach what you do in this business. Whatever you want your team to do, first start doing that yourself.

Most of you, by now, must have understood that many Network Marketing Companies offer Residual Income to its distributors. Such income occurs on the efforts that you've already put forth. Residual income is possible only when your network continues to generate repeat sales. This is the reason many professionals get attracted to Network Marketing Business.

You build this business once and enjoy the fruits for many years to come. Therefore, it becomes more important to understand the products of the business and educate your team the same. When they start believing in the product and have knowledge about the products, they generate repeat sale. Equally important is to identify a Network Marketing Company which offers revolutionary products and services that no other company can match. This will help in continued sales and hence you will continue to get residual income.

When the products are of unmatching quality, your team will not have to make huge efforts to sell. They just need to equip themselves with the right information and knowledge; sales will happen automatically. People will come to you to buy products. When instead of sale, you have a solution to offer, people will surely buy from you.

➤ I don't sell, people buy from me.

Progress made so far

Technological advancements and innovation have led to many companies creating breakthrough products and services. Distribution is slowly and steadily shifting its share from Physical Distribution to Intellectual Distribution. In physical distribution, the customer already knows about the product and goes to the market to buy that product.

The customer already knows what he is going to buy at the time of entering the store. Whereas in intellectual distribution, the company creates a new product and then creates a need in the mind of the customer as to why they need that product. Once the customers understand the need, they buy the product. In a way, intellectual distribution is far more ahead than physical distribution.

I'm sure in the coming years, more and more such products will be offered to the customers. The customer seeks the solution. In Network Marketing Business, many companies have such a product line and surely they will go a long way going forward.

Understanding the Products

When you've decided to grow big time in this business, you need to master the products. The best place is your own house. Your house should be like a showcase of your products. When your team visits your house, they should indeed feel the importance and significance of using the products. You're a role model for them.

The first circle that you need to perfect is your own. Get knowledge about each category and products. For each product, you must know three things called the FUB of products, namely Features, Usage and Benefits. Understand the unique selling point (USP) of each product.

Your company would provide adequate training programs from time to time about each of its products and it's imperative for you to attend those sessions and take notes. When you do that, your team will follow you and do the same.

While there's no replacement for the classroom training programs, in this age of social media and internet, more and more companies are making use of tools such as Apps,

YouTube, Facebook, Instagram, Zoom and various other mediums to impart knowledge about products.

These are useful tools and you should make ample use of them to promote products to your customers and team. You must encourage your team to use these tools and grow their business. You need to conduct special training sessions with the help of the company to educate your team about such applications and their usage.

> In Network Marketing Business, you're the brand ambassador of your business and products.

Hence, you need to be equipped with the right information and tools about the products of the company. Your success is dependent upon the quantum and quality of knowledge that your team possesses. For that, you need to prepare yourself as the master trainer for your team.

Self-Use of Products

If you're new to the Network Marketing Business, the first thing you can do for which you don't need any outside support is to start using the products that your company offers. Self-Use is critical to success in this business. It enhances your belief in the products. When your team visits your home, their belief level also goes up. When you start using the products at your home, you become the customer of your own business. It is also called selling to own self.

In Network Marketing Business, this small step can create mammoth impact on your organisation. All you need is to have a team and replicate the same habit in your team. Some people think that they have to go door-to-door to sell these products. I would be the last person on this earth had it been the case.

This business is all about creating users in every home. Self-use has great power. It seems a very small gesture, but it has a multiplier effect. Imagine thousands of homes of your team using the products for their own use. The sales volume will go sky-rocketing. Sometimes the new persons in the team may think that he would start using the products when they have a team. This is quite obvious. There comes the importance of counselling again. Teach them the importance of self-use and the duplication concept.

One has to be taught the basics right from the beginning. This is the first step. New Distributors Orientation Program (NDOP) is conducted only for new business owners where they are taught these baby steps.

Demo Bag - Your Powerhouse Tool

One demonstration is equal to a thousand words spoken because what you see, you believe more. Demonstration of products is essential for your growth in this business. As we discussed earlier, every product has Features, Usage and Benefits, you need to show the products to your prospects so that they can touch and feel them.

When during the presentation, you show a demo of the products, they are an eye-opener. I've seen prospects' eyes lit up when they see the demo. So, in order to make your presentation livelier and more effective, incorporate a few product demos in it. In your PASE meetings, you need to learn how to demonstrate the products. Make notes of those demos in your notebook. Once you've noted down the demos, practice them at your home so that you gain confidence.

Self-use also significantly enhances your belief about the quality of the products. When you go out and show the business presentation to your prospects, you need to show them product demos as well. For that, you need to prepare a demo bag which contains product broachers, leaflets, product booklet, demo-kit, a file containing testimonials, newspaper cuttings and established research papers relating to the products.

Your demo bag is the powerhouse tool of your business. It should be professionally managed and attractive looking. Leaflets and product booklets should be new. Your demo kit should include all the products for which you're showing the demo and other items needed. Try to bring everything along with you in your demo bag rather than asking for things from the prospect's house.

Make your demos effective by supplying relevant testimonial videos, product videos and research papers. These things enhance the credibility about the products and business.

The sooner you start showing the demos the better it is. Check with your growing upline and take their help in getting your demo bag ready. I've personally experienced that demo of products raises the belief of the prospect immensely. Sometimes they get into the business because they saw the eye-opening demonstration of products.

Make use of this tool and learn to duplicate the same in your teams. Remember that no business presentation is complete without showing a demonstration of the products.

Magic-Corner for Products

Since most of the networkers in the network marketing business operate from home, it becomes imperative for them to understand that their home should be an example for others both in terms of leadership and products. There should be visibility of the products of your company in your home to demonstrate that you're loyal towards the company and the products.

> ➤ You should've a dedicated place in your home where you can exhibit the products that you deal in. It can be over the refrigerator or a special corner for placing the products. It will create magic in your business; that is why it is named Magic-Corner.

People around you must understand the intensity of your dedication towards the business. It enhances your self-image and posture. Magic-Corner helps in retailing the products to people who are not in your business but want to use the products. Magic-Corner is a useful tool to do product training for new distributors.

Product Training

Training is an integral part of your business. Since a successful network marketing business can only be built if the product line is trending and people need those products, you need to train first yourself and then your team about the products. For this training plays a vital role.

You need to create a second, third and further tier of leaders who can train their teams about the products. Make use of the training sessions provided by the company through classroom training or online training programs. Read the brochures and leaflets of the company and master the products.

Over the years, I've conducted countless training programs for my teams across India to educate the teams about the usage of the products. Now there are so many leaders doing the same thing for the organization. That's the power of the duplication.

We use various training programs depending upon the need of the team at various stages of their growth. For new people who have recently joined or are about to make a decision, we conduct Cover Dish at the house of an existing distributor and invite 4-5 couples to their home and eat together and discuss the products and business.

This is a very effective method of informal teaching and relationship building. People share their experience and feedback about the products and the business and new people get an insight into the same. Every week we conduct PASE (Product and System Education) Meetings where we use the platform to create a new tier of leaders who discuss the products and system.

PASE Meetings are an extremely useful tool for developing leaders in the organization. It serves manifold purposes. In a month, we do NDOP (New Distributors Orientation Program) to meet and train all the new people who joined our business within the last 30 days. Besides this, we do product camps, product workshops, Live Demos, special SPA Sessions and weekly morning get-togethers for product training sessions and relationship building.

Using Modern Technological Tools

We conduct webinars and video sessions using applications such as Zoom, Skype, etc. to hold product training sessions for the long-distance groups. I would highly encourage you to make use of these tools for effective communication with your outstation teams. Using online tools, create leaders in your outstation teams who can conduct product training sessions for local groups. Always remember that for products, touch and feel is important. Arrange local training classes for your outstation teams where they can meet with the trainer personally and also touch and feel the products.

I have had the privilege of conducting my "Train the Trainer" program, both online and offline, which has helped many young entrepreneurs. They are now independently handling big teams and developing a sustainable business. Training is a continuous process in organizational development. Make your training sessions effective and interesting so that new people in your team get attached to them and grow in the business. Use interactive ideas and role plays to make your training program engaging and entertaining.

I've observed leaders of many Network Marketing Companies and found out that they all put great emphasis on training and education. Success in Network Marketing Business is directly proportional to the level of knowledge and training of your teams. At the bottom of all this is your personal grooming. You need to perfect your circle first then only you can train others.

Just to recapitulate....

- Everyone is a salesman selling some product or service. It is deep-rooted in us. People take selling indifferently. In Network Marketing Business, some people are really good at selling the products while some are good at sponsoring new people. It is a balancing act.

- Technology has brought about a transformational change in the products and services. Competition has become more intense. The needs and expectations of the customer are also changing fast. The customer is not more informed and educated. The customer has many choices.

- Methods of sales also need to be changed with changing times. New skills need to be acquired. Understanding the USP of the product helps in pitching the product to the customer. Learn the features, usage and benefit of each product.

- Self-use is a small but very significant step in developing a big business.

- Product Training is a continuous process. You and your team need to participate in all such training programs whether online or offline. The more the training, the more the sales volume.

- In this business, product demonstration makes the sales process easy and simple. One demo is equal to a thousand words. Demos are eye-openers. Promote Demo bags/kits in your team. No sales presentation is complete without a demonstration.

- Make a dedicated magic-corner in your house. It is an effective tool. Magic corner helps in letting people see, touch and feel the products. It helps in the retailing of products to your near and dear ones.

- PASE Meetings and NDOP help new people understand the range of products, how to use them and their demonstration.

- Modern tools are very helpful in making presentations to outstation teams. Train your teams for using the tools like webinars, video calls and other applications.

Scribble your Notes

CHAPTER 11

Objection Handling

Pretend that every single person
you meet has a sign around his
or her neck that says, "Make me
feel important." Not only will you
succeed in sales, but you will
also succeed in life.

-MARY KAY ASH

Objection handling is the most delicate yet important learning in sales, doesn't matter whether it is a traditional business model or Direct Selling model. Wherever any sale is happening, objections are bound to arise.

Why did I say that it is a delicate subject? Why do we say handling?

It's because only on delicate things we write "Handle with care". Raising objections is not bad and neither is receiving objections. All you need to do is to prepare yourself for receiving the objection and learning the techniques of handling those objections in the best possible manner and meeting the overall objective of closing the sale.

This is the most crucial part of the sales process and most often than not, the difference between a successful sale and a failed sale is how you handled the objections.

All Objections are not bad or negative

Let's first handle the issue that why all objections aren't bad. As a salesperson, you may not want your prospect or customer to raise any objection, but that is a peculiar and unique scenario, unlikely to happen. There will be no learning in that and you may get stuck up in the next sale. So, don't run away from objections.

Prepare yourself for receiving those objections and handling them with care. Whenever your prospect is raising an objection, it doesn't necessarily mean that they're against you or are negative. Instead, the prospect is with you and participative in the sales process as I have told you that objections are an integral part of sales.

The prospect has the legitimate right of raising objections and by raising the objection, they are exercising that right. This also means that the prospect is listening to you and may be keen to buy your product or service. All they want is that you satisfy the query. Once you have done that, you're inching closer to clinching the sale.

Why does the prospect raise objections?

Well, it may not be necessary for you to know the reasons for raising the objections because it depends purely on the psychology of the prospect on that particular day. It's not in your control either. There can be a number of reasons because of which a prospect raises objections.

It's also possible that the objection being raised by the prospect may not be the real objection. They may be hiding the real objection deep inside their heart and present you an altogether different objection. You need to be ready with the right tools and techniques to reach that hidden objection. As you go further and read the chapter, you will find enough tools that will equip you to face the objections with full confidence.

How to deal with objections

Those who don't prepare themselves beforehand, will feel butterflies in the stomach in front of the prospect. Preparation is key to your success in dealing with the objections. Most of the objections are common in nature and hence they are frequently asked. You need to get answers to all those objections and start rehearsing to encounter them.

Attend all the meetings and seminars of the business because this topic is discussed in detail at such forums. You can also listen and watch the audio and videos of successful leaders who will guide you in dealing with objections and how to handle them.

In your PASE meetings and team meetings, conduct mock drills and role-plays to have a real-time feel of how to handle the objections. Such meetings are a great platform where new persons in the business get hands-on knowledge about what the different types of objections are and how to handle them.

You may even write down all the objections and try to figure out what are the possible and alternative solutions that have been discussed in the meeting. Collect all relevant testimonials and research material and file them properly. It is a great tool in your hands when you go out to meet your prospects. Testimonial videos of products are very useful in handling product related objections. You can give a copy of the research paper to the prospect to read it at home.

When you are new in the business, try to spend as much time at your disposal to be with your successful upline. It is immensely beneficial. Watch them doing all the things in the business. Watch them carefully how they handle the objections of the prospects.

When your upline is doing meetings for you, listen to them and watch their posture, body language and how they listen and handle the queries of the prospects. It is a great learning tool.

I normally use the following process to handle the objection.

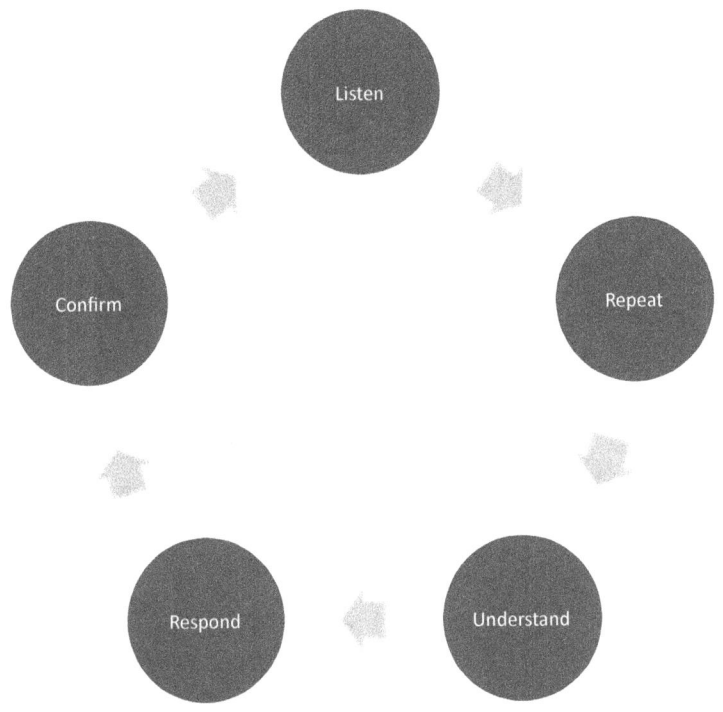

These steps fully satisfy the objections raised by the prospect. Listening is an art that needs to be developed. It can fetch wonderful results. Once the prospect has raised certain objection, you can put forth some smart questions just to confirm whether you have listened to the prospect correctly or not. It also helps in establishing a rapport with the prospect by letting him know that you're listening. Once you have clearly understood the objection raised by the prospect, you need to respond.

I'll discuss how you can respond in different ways. Then you need to confirm whether the prospect has understood your response or not.

Important Steps in Handling Objections

1. Active and patient listening

Your prospects are the important individuals to close the sale. They are the ones who will make the final decision. When they are a bit apprehensive and raising certain objections, your role is to listen to them with apt attention. Listen well during that period, maintain eye-to-eye contact and nod your head in between to make your prospect feel that you're actively listening. This satisfies their ego.

It doesn't matter whether you've listened to that objection a number of times before, but this is a new prospect and you need to show them due respect while they're explaining the objection. You will be able to answer and resolve the query raised by your prospect only when you've listened to it with full attention. When you do this, it makes your prospect comfortable. It's been widely researched that listening is a key ingredient for high performing teams. Listening is a great art. Practise it.

When your prospect is speaking and you're listening, you need to have a copy and a pen in your hand and write down key points of the objection. This is significantly important and creates an instant rapport with the prospect. Make sure you've well understood the objection raised by the prospect; you may raise a follow-up question at the end just to reconfirm what was said. Write down all the objections, one by one, raised by the prospect. Don't ask for more. Just let the prospect speak out. Once it's over, draw a straight line at the end. Ask a question to your prospect. If I answer all your objections to your satisfaction, then would you be interested to join the business?

2. Sometimes Questions are the Answers

Sometimes, asking questions is the best method of handling an objection. The important thing is when and what to ask. This technique can't be used to handle all the objections but wherever it works, it works effectively. Instead of answering the objection raised by the prospect, sometimes it's effective to ask a question back and let the prospect give the answer to it. It's called sending the ball to the opposite court. Let me give you a sample for this technique.

When the prospect says, "I don't have time to do this business," you may ask a question, "Will you have time two years from now considering your busy schedule?" "Did you have time two years ago?" Obviously, the prospect will say "No". Now you did not answer the prospect, rather the prospect answered their question themselves.

I'll give you a real-time example of a question-answer technique that I generally do with my prospects.

When the prospect says, "The products are very expensive."

I ask a follow-up question, "Do you want to get rich?"

He says, "Yes, but the products are expensive."

Then I ask another question, "What do you think, which coffee is cheaper; the one that is sold at a railway platform by a local vendor or the cup of coffee at a coffee shop?"

He answers, "Of course, the one at the railway platform." Then I ask, "Who is selling more coffee?" His answer is again the same that more coffee is sold at the railway platforms in comparison to coffee shops.

My next question is, "Who is rich?" Now he says, "The coffee shop owner."

I ask him," Why is it so?"

The coffee shop owner is selling a costly cup of coffee and also selling a smaller number of coffees compared to that being sold at the railway platform but still he's richer than the local vendor.

Then I make the final punch.

I ask him, "By the way, where would you prefer to go with your wife for a cup of coffee?"

His obvious choice would be the coffee shop. I persist, "If you would like to start your own coffee selling business, which one would you prefer?"

He again answers coffee shop. Then I say that's the answer to your objection.

The cup of coffee that is served by the lounge assistant in a coffee shop has quality. They use the finest source of coffee beans and use quality ingredients. The lounge has a pleasant ambience, comfortable sitting and the assistant serves with a smile. Quality can never be cheap. You've to pay the price for the quality.

If you ask a series of such questions and let the prospect answer it, there's a greater likelihood that they'll join your business. This technique has been remarkably explained by the best-selling author Allen Pease in his book "Questions are the Answers."

3. Ascertaining and finding the hidden objection

Sometimes the prospect may not let you know the real objection and present before you some other objection. He may just evade to let you know the real objection. When the prospect has put forth all the objections and still, I feel that they're not letting me know the real reason, I ask them a simple question.

I ask, "**In addition to that,** is there anything else which is stopping you in taking the decision of joining this business?"

This phrase 'In addition to that' works effectively to bring out the real objection out of the customer. You may persist until you reach the hidden objection. This is a tricky technique but surely effective.

When you reach to the real hidden objection and provide your prospect with the solution for the same, there's every chance of you bringing that prospect in the business. The real purpose of handling objection is to understand what your prospect needs and letting them know how that need can be fulfilled through this business.

4. Feel, felt, found

These three words are probably the best three words that I've learnt in people skills and objection handling while building the business in the last twenty years. This is the masterstroke in dealing with people without hurting their ego. I wish I had learnt this during my long studying career. Nevertheless, as I've said earlier, the things that you learn here will make you feel good in every aspect and sphere of life. Let's first understand the thumb rule of skill with people, which is very useful in objection handling.

➢ Never disagree with people upfront.

Every person who is sitting in front of you as your prospect has his/her own ego. When we tell them that they're wrong, it hurts them and they sit in opposition to you. I'm not saying you agree to whatever wrong they are saying, but there has to be a more refined way of saying without disturbing their ego. Always first agree to disagree. It will help you a lot.

Feel, felt and found is the golden rule for replying and handling an objection. It's a proven technique which makes your prospect think the way you want them to think. First, I will explain to you how to structure these three words in the form of statements.

> Tell your prospect, "I understand how you feel." This shows two things. One, you have listened to them carefully and second, you sympathise with them.
> Tell the prospect that either you or someone else felt the same way as them initially. This satisfies the customer that they are not the only ones thinking that way. At the same time, the word 'initially' conveys them the message that things can change.
> Tell your prospect that you later found that you were satisfied and got what you wanted.

Let me take an example to explain to you how these three statements work. Suppose the prospect says that the products are costly. Now, never say that they're wrong, I will prove that through a demo. This will dissatisfy their ego. Let us build the right structure using the three statements.

The template:

> *Dear, I understand how you feel that the products are costly and there are cheaper products available in the market. I, along with many of my friends who are successful in this business felt the same way initially, but when we started using the products, we found that the cost per use was very less, the products were of top quality and on top of it, these products fulfilled many of our dreams.*

Then you may quote an example and do a price comparison.

There is a huge difference between knowing something and mastering something. You need to master these techniques and that will happen when you do more and more objection handling sessions sitting in front of your prospect.

5. Kill the person with knowledge

I always tell my teams that you can kill a person with knowledge. The Network Marketing Business will bring you the expertise of highly successful networkers who're successful not only in this business but also in their traditional life.

You'll have access to all their knowledge and wisdom. They can guide you with what exactly works and what not. You need to get the right knowledge and apply it. When you provide your prospect with the right information at the right time and in the right manner, you have nailed them. Mark my words.

I have seen many networkers not learning the things and facing lots of challenges whereas some have a smooth sail. When you use the right body language, posture and deliver the right solution to the prospect, you increase your chances of success.

As I said earlier, you need to perfect only one circle and that's your own. When the prospect sees the spark in you, they'll get attached to you. You need to become a magnetic leader. The good news is you can be one.

6. Need not handle all the objections

Leaders share their experiences that when you handle a couple of objections effectively, that satisfies the prospect and they no longer want to get solutions to all the objections raised. You needn't handle all the objections.

Learn and get expertise in the techniques and make them your routine. When these techniques run through your blood, you become a magnet. The objective of the prospect isn't to test you on all the objections. They understand that you've the guts to be the captain of the ship and would help them sail through and achieve their dreams and goals.

7. Closing the deal

Once you observe that the prospect is satisfied with your responses, your next million-dollar statement should be, "Let's start the business now."

I don't know why people don't make this most important statement. Closing the sale is the most important concluding step. You must close the deal there and then only. If still the prospect does something dilly-dally, give them some literature to study or some audio to listen to and book the next appointment. Never close the door on anybody.

Handling objections during a presentation

As you grow up in Network Marketing Business and have more faith in the company, products, system and above all on yourself, it'll start reflecting in your presentation skills. The best time to handle most of the objections upfront is while doing the presentation of the business plan and the demonstration of products.

If your expertise is in doing that, you need not face those objections from the prospect during the follow-up. Taking a hypothetical scenario, you can handle objections in your presentation. The prospect gets the answers to most of them and can move further from there. This is a skill that you can acquire.

Most of the price objections can effectively be handled while giving a demonstration of the products. The benefit is that the prospect is seeing the demo and at the same time understanding the quality, price and effectiveness of the products. Watch your upline as they do the same during their presentations and learn to present the same kind of presentation.

Common objections faced in Network Marketing Business and tips to overcome them

This business is not for me

These are the people who haven't fully understood the potential and the rewards that this business offers. They pretend that they're quite satisfied with their present job or profession. You needn't argue with these people. Show them the success of your business and briefly explain to them the quality of people that are already successful in the business. Show them the big picture. Respect their professional ego. Connect them to some successful leaders of your business.

I don't have time

Ask them a question. Is it a problem or an achievement? If it's a problem, you need to find the solution. This business can offer them a solution. This business is 5 years Vs 45 years plan. Many people have achieved significant success in this business by building this business alongside their job or profession in part-time.

The return on time invested (ROTI) is quite high in the network marketing business. As a busy person, you know the importance and value of time more than others and you can better invest your time in this business to create a permanent source of income and financial security for your family. Focus on Time, Money and Financial Security that this business can offer.

Show them the success of the business and what leaders have achieved. Give examples of leaders who have retired early through the business.

I don't have money

Tell them that's why they need this business more than anyone else. This business is the solution to the money crisis. Network marketing has many stories of people building the business from rags to riches. Tell them that you don't need money to build this business, you need dreams.

If you've a dream, you can achieve success in this business. Network marketing business is ideally suited for people who want to start their own business but don't have money. There are examples of students and housewives who have built a big business but initially they started for some pocket money. You can earn handsome profits by retailing the products.

Is it a pyramid scheme?

Many people have bad experiences of someone close to them burning their fingers in fraudulent pyramid schemes. Guidelines laid by Government of India in the year 2016 have put to rest all such companies and declared their business void. Your effort is in making them understand the ethics and principles of the network marketing business and how it has helped millions achieve their dreams and goals.

There are quality people from different fields who have taken a decision to build the business and their decision carries some weight. Assure your prospects that if such people are building this business, they must've taken a thoughtful decision.

Those who joined earlier succeeded

The best time to build this business is now. Everything is set for these businesses to explode. The purpose of writing this book is to make you aware that there is a tsunami of networkers and many new companies are starting operations.

> ➢ If there's any best time to build the network marketing business, it's now.

Both the industry and the government are thriving hard for entrepreneurial development. It is slated that this industry can create the maximum number of entrepreneurs. Now, Network Marketing Companies have backing from the government guidelines and they're investing heavily in creating infrastructure and bringing new product lines.

I know someone who has failed in Network Marketing

My counter-question to them softly is, "Do you know any field where someone has not failed? Why so specific about network marketing business alone?" People never say that I'll not make my child an engineer because some engineer has failed. People fail everywhere and people succeed everywhere. We need to be sure about ourselves. Everybody has their own set of reasons to fail or succeed.

If you dig in, work hard and commit yourself for two to three years, there's every possibility that you'll succeed here. The decision lies with you. It's your decision. In case of any eventuality, only you're there for your family and not someone else. So, the decision should also be yours. You need to understand the potential of the business and what it can provide to you. If you've a dream and a desire, you can achieve that here.

Products are expensive

I discussed this objection in detail in the previous chapter on products. Usually, this objection occurs when the prospect hasn't seen the product demonstration and application. Use 'feel, felt and found' technique to make them realize that products are of great quality, per usage cost is low and above all, these products offer us a business opportunity.

By using and promoting these products, you can become a celebrity, travel the world over and enjoy on the beaches of the world. Make them touch and feel the products. Do price comparisons. Explain to them the money-back guarantee that your company offers. Assure them about the quality and international standards that the company follows in making of these products.

You can handle any objection that comes your way when you've the right skillset learnt and practised. Associate with successful leaders and watch them handle the objections with the prospect. In my twenty years of experience in the Network Marketing Industry, on countless occasions, I've dealt with objections sitting right in front of the prospect. I've also dealt with the objections while speaking on this topic with my teams at different forums.

Believe me, objections are raised by the prospect because they really want to clear the air on certain things objecting in their minds. Once you clear the air, the prospect is ready to sign in your business. You need to be a patient listener and quickly gauge what your prospect is intending to convey to you. This all comes with practice. This is what the learning curve is all about. When you spend time in this business, you rise on the learning curve and your efficiency and productivity increases.

Just to recapitulate....

➲ Objection handling is an important step in any sales whether it is the traditional sale or closing the sale in Network Marketing Business. It needs to be handled with care. First, understand that all objections are neither bad nor negative.

➲ The purpose of raising an objection is that the prospect is interested in the sale but wants further information.

➲ The objection is not that big a problem. The problem lies in dealing with the objection. It's here that people commit mistakes. Handling the objection is a step-by-step procedure that can be learnt by observing successful leaders doing the same with the prospect.

➲ Listening is the most important phase of the entire objection handling process. When your prospect is raising the objection, you need to listen patiently with apt attention.

➲ In many cases, questions can be raised to answer a question. This is quite an effective technique for handling an objection.

➲ Finding the hidden objection is the pertinent task. Ask the prospect if they have some other objection in addition to this.

➲ Feel, Felt and Found are magical words that can handle any objection. Master these three words.

➲ Most of the objections are frequently asked questions. You know beforehand what the prospect is going to ask.

Scribble your Notes

Recommended Books for Reading

- "Find your Why" by Simon Sinek
- "Question are the Answers" by Allan Pease
- "The 21 Irrefutable Laws of Leadership" by John C Maxwell
- "The Parable of The Pipeline" by Burke Hedges
- "Becoming A Person of Influence" by John C Maxwell and Jim Dornan
- "Rich Dad's Cashflow Quadrant" by Robert T Kiyosaki
- "Goals!" by Brian Tracy
- "How I raised myself from Failure to Success in Selling" by Frank Bettger
- "How to win friends and influence people" by Dale Carnegie
- "Selling to win" by Richard Denny
- "Be a winner everytime" by Promod Batra
- "Discover your Destiny" by Robin Sharma